HR You Can Use!

Answers to the 5 issues keeping business owners up at night

Lori Kleiman, SPHR

HR You Can Use!

Answers to the 5 issues keeping business owners up at night

ISBN-13: 978-1495986567
ISBN-10: 149598656X

 HR Topics Publishing
Glenview, IL
lori@hrtopics.com
www.hrtopics

Printed in the United States of America

Acknowledgements

A career in human resources is born from years of education, experiences, patience, exasperation, ambition and study of the human spirit. The interaction of people and business has always been fascinating to me, and sharing how to make that intersection work in small business has allowed me to create a career of passion and growth.

With the support of my husband – Andy Korn – I set off on my entrepreneurial journey in 1998 and established HRpartners. Our mission was to provide HR services for organizations too small to have their own HR. I could not have undertaken such a journey without the confidence Andy had that my enterprise would be the success it was. When clients were scare, he would listen as I worried, but never suggested I "get a real job". He would wait patiently until the next client or project came along. It was a ten-year journey that we took together; and we continue today as I embark on the next enterprise of speaking and writing. The partnership we share is golden and goes far beyond entrepreneurial businesses.

It's not easy growing up today in any circumstance – but imagine your childhood when a business is being run from your home! Libby, Marjorie, and Adam dealt with a home where employees took over the basement. They often returned from school to find conferences occurring at the kitchen table. They never knew what supplies were for school projects and which were for the next client presentation. Somehow they allowed us to operate a full service consulting firm - and managed to grown up to become three amazing adults. Thanks to the three of you for your patience,   flexibility, and confidence that maybe this once mom did know what she was doing!

And to those employees that put up with working from my home – you will never be forgotten. Julie, Rebecca, and Deepti were so patient with the kids, cat, kitchen redesign, and illness that we all lived through together. Not to leave out Saundra....rarely around the office, but always around in spirit. My sister Debbie became the ruler of the roost – whether family or HRpartners related, she always took care of anything someone needed. All would agree HRpartners would not have flourished had she not been diligent to provide all the tools we needed for success. Without the five of you, the career path I took would have never have had the successes it has. I will always have fond memories of what we have built together.

Make new friends but keep the old, one is silver and the other gold...the adage we are all familiar with. The adage is personified in my friend Annie Rutherford. She spent weeks grading papers for her junior high science classes, only to devote the next two weekends and many evenings editing my second book. And her husband Ross was there for every step helping out. Making my vision a priority is really what friendship is all about.

My father introduced me to the business world at a young age. In my early teen years, I accompanied him to industry conferences and was introduced as the heir apparent. My father, Michael Kleiman, took the time to teach me the world of business, and with that knowledge and a love of people – my career in human resources evolved. I thank my father every day for the business basics I still count on today.

I am lucky to have a cheerleader in my corner that has confidence in anything I decide to undertake. Charlene

Podolsky is more than just a mother; she is a friend with an eye for editing that helps to make my books even a notch better. Without her, each phase of my life would have been taken on a lonely path and likely less successful without her support and guidance.

And so, the story begins. This is the book for all the small business owners that I have met over the years. Some clients, some acquaintances – but all having questions and interest in the puzzle we call human resources. It is my hope that this book will take you on the journey and assure you that you are not alone. All small businesses have HR challenges – together we can share simple and affordable solutions.

Table of Contents

Chapter One   The 5 HR issues facing business   1

Chapter Two   What is Human Resources   7

Chapter Three   Bringing HR into your business   21

Chapter Four   Compliance   53

Chapter Five   Recruiting   73

Chapter Six   Compensation and benefits   87

Chapter Seven   Process and technology   97

Chapter Eight   Outsourcing   107

Chapter Nine   Pulling it all together   127

About the author   133

The 5 HR issues facing business

The focus of this book is to address real concerns small business owners have in the area of human resources. The expertise shared in the text comes from a combination of sixteen years of human resource consulting, twelve years of running a family business, and personal interaction with entrepreneurs, family business owners, and various executives. Furthermore, HR Topics has compiled a propriety survey from more than 400 businesses that helps to reduce the human resources puzzle in small business down to five critical areas that executives need to address. The survey and practical applications will be the baseline for the issues we address in this book.

Our survey was compiled by reflecting on the issues raised and the work conducted with business owners and executives in the past twenty years. We continue to gather data and allow the survey to grow as businesses evolve and face new challenges in the twenty first century. The survey has nationwide participation, and includes businesses from various sectors of organizational enterprise including non-profit, manufacturing, professional services, education, construction, and travel. The average business size of survey respondents was 73 employees, with a median number of employees of 176. The difference between the average and the median further highlights the diversity of participation from family businesses and start-ups, as well as publically traded and larger operations. The participants are all organizations with operations based in the United States regardless of the ownership structure. Some participants have foreign owners, but the complexity of global human resources is not one we will address here.

The survey's diversity reflects the organizations that comprise the small and middle market business community in the United States. The vast majority of the participants are successful enterprises with great value provided to organization stakeholders and their local communities. For the purposes of this book, we will define small business as the number of employees being fewer than 300. In many cases, the organizations included in the survey had fewer than 50 employees, but still faced the issues of their large-scale competitors.

The 5 HR issues facing business

The survey identifies the main issues as follows:

- Who should be responsible for HR
- Compliance
- Recruiting and Retention
- Compensation and Benefits
- Processes of HR

The goal of this book is to explore the issues raised in the survey. These are tactical issues that must be faced by all business owners and executives on both a functional and administrative level. It is simply impossible to run your business without understanding the impact of these five topics.

To allow for accurate benchmarking of your situation against the survey, the results have been broken down into size of the organization. The categories have been determined based on various HR laws that impact organizations at different sizes.

Top HR issues facing business owners

	Number of employees			
	Under 20	20 - 49	50 - 99	100 or more
Structure of HR	49.12%	68.09%	51.24%	43.4%
Compliance	33.33%	50.0%	49.59%	42.77%
Recruiting and retention	29.82%	18.09%	12.4%	14.47%
Compensation and Benefits	5.26%	5.32%	9.92%	16.35%
Processes of HR	5.26%	9.57%	6.61%	11.32%

Given the depth of participation, we are confident these are issues and processes you are trying to incorporate into your organization. We will show a variety of options that should meet the needs of your HR issues, from improving your current in house options to outsourcing the entire function. There are many options that will go beyond the necessity of adding a full-time resource to your payroll. Solutions discussed should be shared with your management team as well as tips that strip away the complexity of certain issues. We designate portions in the text that suggest conversations to have with your management team about how a particular aspect of HR is being handled today.

In addition to the issues identified in the survey, we have added a chapter on what it means to outsource the HR function. Outsourcing can be an effective solution for small businesses. Business owners have many questions and concerns about how outsourcing can benefit their organization we will attempt to answer. As you will see in chapter eight, there are options for business that are affordable and will allow you to retain your corporate culture and identity.

Legend used throughout the book

The field of human resources is ever changing. At the same time, the processes and procedures of employee management must be customized to an organizations culture, location, industry, and financial situation. Access to the best way to incorporate the concepts of our information can be attained in a number of ways. Certain concepts may require further analysis or a conversation with your internal leadership team, others require outside expertise or training. Where you see these symbols, you can access resources as appropriate to help accomplish your goals:

COMPANION TOOL: Our supplemental material provides tools allowing the business leader or HR administrator to implement the suggestions in the text. HR Topics provides "how to" solutions and webinars in a format that will allow you to customize the suggestions to your organization. The workbook is available on our website, www.hrtopics.com

INTERNET ASSISTANCE: Compliance will often vary from location to location and based on the size of the organization. Compliance situations that may have different meanings for different businesses are indicated with this icon. We recommend you refer to the Internet for the most up-to-date or geographic-specific information.

SHOP TALK: Organizations have many moving pieces relating to employee interaction. This symbol indicates questions that should be asked of your internal team or trusted advisors for verification and clarification on how you have embraced the issue being discussed. Executives can use this information to evaluate the processes and ensure they are comfortable with the answers.

Chapter Two

What is Human Resources

Human Resources, as we know it today, is the grandchild of the human relations movement. The study of employees in the workplace began in the early 20th century with pioneering work striving to improve economic efficiency in manufacturing jobs. The industrial scientists of the time focused on the principal inputs of the process — labor — that sparked others to look more closely at workforce productivity.

Another pioneer in the study of workplace labor was Elton Mayo, whose Hawthorne Studies documented how employees reacted when they were provided with various stimuli. Mayo's research found that when employees were the focus of attention, productivity suddenly increased. The Hawthorne studies revealed that attention and engagement paid to employees, more than financial compensation and working conditions, yielded more productive workers. This was the initial impetus for the creation of departments focused on the employee.

In the mid-twentieth century, the position of personnel administrator was created in many manufacturing operations. Decades later the same group became the human resources departments that we are familiar with today. The early personnel departments were very administrative in nature: their primary focus was meeting the needs of the employees and providing administrative services for the organization. While this is still a necessary part of the human resources function, today's HR leaders look to focus on alignment between the employees and the strategic goals of their organization.

Today, highly successful organizations consider the chief human resources officer a critical member of the leadership team. It is the CHRO's responsibility to drive business initiatives forward and ensure corporate programs are sustainable. In smaller organizations, the HR leader may not be an executive level position, but should be charged with the responsibility of aligning business goals with employee actions. We continuously see high-performing organizations that consider recruiting, retention, and development of top talent as a component of the strategic plan.

The results of our survey demonstrate the five critical human resources issues facing executives shown in chapter one. These issues divert attention from the sales and operational efforts that will your drive business forward. Overwhelmingly, executives have found there is no clear path for help in solving these issues. They don't have budgets to hire consultants, and calling their labor attorney with every question becomes expensive very quickly. Most importantly, we hear that managers simply "don't know what they don't know" in many HR situations. It can take hours of research to find the answer to a situation a high-level HR professional would be able to answer quickly. Having an ongoing, straightforward solution to human resource concerns is a critical problem to be solved for business owners.

Human Resources is relevant to all businesses

CEOs and CFOs do their best to stay on top of employment law and HR processes, but the rules change frequently. Municipalities and industries have specific guidelines that must be addressed. A great deal of human resources decision making is impacted by case law and precedent handed down in the courts. This makes for a tangled web to navigate when your core competency is based in another area of the business. Executives need to be confident that someone has their back when it comes to human resources.

To provide a baseline for comparison, let's review the benchmark ratio of the size of an HR department to total employee population. Data from the Society for Human Resource Management "Trend Survey of 2013" finds that the average organization has one HR team member for every 133 employees. This is a decrease from approximately thirty years ago when we had one HR team member for every 100 employees. The reduction in headcount of the HR function can be attributed to economic necessity, availability of outsourced vendors for administration, such as 401(k) administrators and payroll processing, and the technological advances that are available to organizations of all sizes. This ratio is a generalization for all organizations; your appropriate HR needs will change based on factors such as education, location, technical ability, and fluency of your workforce. The number might also fluctuate based on functions that are outsourced through HR vendors such as benefits, training, and recruiting.

If your organization is smaller than 133 employees, HR activities cannot be ignored. While HR may not warrant a full-time position in your organization, it is likely taking valuable time away from your leadership team. As we see in the survey, even organizations that are quite small will find that HR functionality diverts attention from the leaders. Talk to your leadership team about where they think they are spending time on activities that are considered human resources in nature.

Keep the 133 employee-to-HR function ratio in mind as a guide. Once your organization becomes a size where employee issues begin to take the attention of management you may want to begin evaluation. The key is to consider the impact of your current HR function and determine how HR will be addressed in your organization in the future. If you currently have a small base of employees you will likely address the HR function by utilizing alternatives to the full-time, in house human resources department.

Bringing professional HR in too early can be harmful. This can be a waste of money, time, and resources for the organization. You don't need an HR function that is spending the day creating new procedures, meeting vendors you are unlikely to retain in the future, having another conversation with managers on employee performance, and creating initiatives that distract the leadership. There have been many HR administrators that fill their day with discounts for employees, writing reports and other tasks that simply to do not add value or help meet your organizational goals.

Metrics that determine the effectiveness of HR

Metrics are the key to effective operational management. In human resources, we look to metrics that impact productivity and improve the bottom line profitability of the organization on a regular basis. Many of these will help us determine whether human resource expertise would be valuable to an organization. Common indicators that point to additional attention to being paid to human resources activities include:

- Expansion plans for next 12 to 18 months

- Turnover levels that take extensive time to manage

- Communication from regulatory entities about compliance

- High unemployment rate

- Percentage of annual goal completion by management team

- Non-uniform policies among departments or locations

- Areas of annual budget that impact employee interactions

- CFO or controller saying that it's time to rethink HR

Reviewing these metrics with a critical eye will help you determine whether HR needs additional attention in your organization.

Deciding whether you need HR

The leadership team should evaluate when there are trivial issues bubbling to the top or taking critical management time. Some examples of this might include approving time off, entering basic data into the payroll system, conducting benefit enrollment meetings, etc. The need to divert more attention to employment matters and away from critical areas of expertise will indicate the time has come to bring HR into your organization. Whether you add a new resource or find a partner to address the issues, the idea is to redirect the current responsibilities to a skilled professional who is able to understand your needs.

We often see that the HR function in smaller organizations is even more critical given the complexity of compliance, recruiting, training, and succession planning. One small mistake in these areas can be detrimental in terms of hiring a poor performer or missing a critical compliance deadline. If your management team is focused on growth, someone needs to be accountable for employee development and talent acquisition to ensure the people are in place when your growth occurs. The HR function is commonly addressed as a hybrid function or a function for which outsourcing is a viable option. This is especially true in organizations with fewer than fifty employees. Almost any situation is appropriate, as long as HR is addressed and given priority.

 Discuss the impact of human resources with a trusted advisor who is familiar with your business and your strategy. Business owners typically work closely with an employment or corporate attorney, an accountant, or a CEO roundtable group. Consider reaching out to your payroll service, benefit brokers, and safety vendors. Individuals from these vendors typically have regular interactions with your internal HR activities and can provide insight to the comparative skill level of those employees supporting your HR function. Many of these outside resources will also have relationships with HR consultants and specialists that may be willing to help assess and evaluate your current situation.

Human Resources must be expected to add value

Many leaders of small businesses wonder why they even need someone in HR. Can't managers be responsible for their own people? You may see HR as another expenditure, or another resource that will require your attention. There should be an expectation that HR is not a cost center but will add value to the organization.

Consider what would happen to top line sales if you lose a key salesperson because no one in your organization was aware a competitor was offering an additional week of paid time off. Where would your profit margin go if employees were terminated without proper consideration and evaluation that caused your contribution to unemployment to skyrocket? How do employees on Family and Medical Leave impact overtime in a given department? What is the negative impact on opportunity cost because receivables are taking longer to come in, your operations leader didn't meet with the new vendor, or your shipping team had to overnight a package to a customer? These situations all occur because your managers are busy screening résumés and enrolling new hires into insurance plans – tasks the HR function can handle instead.

While the benefit to the top and bottom line of your budget may not be obvious, employees impact almost every part of your organization. HR is charged with the responsibility of the full life cycle of employment. This begins with finding great candidates and moves through the employment relationship including evaluation, coaching, training, payroll, and benefit management. Finally, we rely on human resources to coach the manager through separations and help employees through the separation process. During the time people are employed by your organization, there are government inquiries, files to be maintained, employee questions, benefits enrollment, and payroll to be processed. HR can add value to the organization by ensuring these are all completed efficiently, cost effectively, and with an eye to your strategic vision.

Anyone can do HR…or NOT!

In small businesses, it's common to find that this mission critical function is given to a team member that has little skill or interest in human resources. It's often the leader of the accounting function. Can you imagine two more diverse personality types than an HR executive and a chief financial officer or controller? While your accounting leader will be capable of learning the HR activities, it is rare that it is a part of their job that will be embraced. Taking on the ownership of the HR function is one thing, but typically your CFO will have to spend more time than necessary finding answers to questions and learning the best practices in human resources administration. There are almost always pressing financial issues, and your CFO's time is generally better spent analyzing reports that will drive the business forward rather than walking new hires through initial paperwork.

Not only is your accounting leader's time taken up unnecessarily, it also affects other leaders within the organization. When there is not a dedicated HR person, managers flounder with HR activities, especially in the areas of hiring and performance management. These tasks take a great deal of time and effort, and for many executives it's a nuisance that takes away from mission-critical activities. Managers generally conclude that it is easier to retain an employee who is "half-a-loaf" rather than going through the work of firing the employee and finding a new team member. Not addressing the performance issue leads to a host of problems: the sub-par employee's efforts may mean re-work is required, overtime is generated when others have to cover for the always absent team member, and a lower quality product goes to your client. These situations chip away at profits, and the reason it happens is simply because no one has the time or interest in managing the employee issues.

As our survey shows, business owners are concerned about human resources issues. Organizations with significantly fewer employees than the benchmark generally won't need a dedicated, full-time human resource employee. However, all organizations need someone with a watchful eye on the HR issues facing the organization. It is critical that the management team align itself with a resource that can provide answers to questions quickly and efficiently. Ownership must have confidence that a trusted professional is watching the human resources function to ensure compliance with relevant legal issues.

Another area to consider is organizational growth. Growth requires careful exploitation of opportunities at a time when it is critical for managers to be focused on their own areas of expertise. Leaders shouldn't be focused on HR activities when growth is part of the strategic plan.

HR departments create rules and push papers

HR is rooted in administration, but whoever is responsible for your HR function should be an interactive business partner to the management team first. Looking at the pyramid, you will see many levels of human resources that make up the typical list of human resources activities.

Understanding where the business is going and how to get there is a key piece in the puzzle of employee management and engagement. Your HR administrator should be a conduit between management and employees to ensure the focus is on business goals at all times.

HR should not be the place where employees can come and whine about their supervisors or policies they don't like for hours on end. Employees must understand that HR is available to talk about workplace situations and provide coaching on topics that relate to the organization and how that might impact their own position. Beyond that, HR is a member of the management team and must focus on the overall benefit of the organization. Your HR team member must understand that it is their obligation to hear what employees are thinking and use that as a way to create new initiatives and ensure that compliance is not compromised. At the same time, your workers need to be at their workstation doing their jobs.

In small organizations, HR will have to weave between all levels of the pyramid on a given day. They must be skilled at administration and strategy, with a foundation in business knowledge to support human resources expertise.

Constantly changing organizations

An organization with staying power is one that's able to adapt to unforeseen changes in the business landscape. This is especially true among smaller organizations as they scan their competition and clients to create new products, services, and evaluate pricing models to carve a place of differentiation in the marketplace. HR should always focus on change management and helping the employees adapt to the direction being identified by management.

Change management may manifest itself in the training needed to prepare high-potential employees for their next roles, dealing with new insurance programs during open enrollment or making changes to policy. HR is charged with the responsibility for communication and integration throughout the organization in each of the changing situations.

Problem solving is a key component to change management and a critical skill to consider in your HR team member. Constant growth brings the opportunity to develop new programs, look for new avenues to recruit team members and provide communication with employees. HR should be aware of changes anticipated and be able to make decisions necessary that address issues in the workplace.

Chapter Three

Bringing HR into your business

It can be difficult for an entrepreneur or small business owner to contemplate adding another department or direct report, especially one that doesn't directly impact sales or generate cost savings. It is not our suggestion that you add human resources simply because it's the thing to do. As with all areas of an operation, there must be a purpose and focus that is closely tied to the organization's mission and goals. Once the leadership team is able to identify this connection, HR will provide a strategic component that impacts both the top and bottom line. As we begin the journey of HR analysis as it relates to your organization, we ask that you keep an open mind to the opportunities that can be created with a formal HR resource.

Small businesses often rely on the relationships of the founder to create and maintain a loyal customer base. As a founder, you may be an innovator, creating the next product that will take your industry by storm, or the salesperson your clients insist on dealing with. Your business is not being driven by employee benefits or processing payroll. You need an HR professional so you can do your job of *working on the business – not in the business*. Your HR professional should be charged with overseeing day-to-day employee relations and addressing situations as they arise.

There are many options when incorporating the HR function into an organization for the first time. Organizations must weigh the options of a dedicated HR professional, utilizing a team member with multiple responsibilities, and department managers responsible for their own people among a few of the choices. They may also elect to outsource human resources activities entirely. In any case, how you embrace HR responsibility should be a thoughtful decision based on the goals of human resources and the culture of the organization.

You may feel that your employees are the driving force of your success. Your strategic plan may call for growth or a change in the mission of the organization. Your business may be knowledge based and rely on top talent to meet the needs of customers and develop new products. In these cases, it is generally preferred to have an HR resource that understands and drives the culture of the business. If your HR person is a direct report to a top executive, there will be an understanding of the preferences of each member of the leadership team. HR can successfully drive human resources decision and actions that work in your culture and with your leadership team.

The human resources solution you select will generally depend on the ability of your employee population to move through the processes generally associated with the HR function independently. For example, in a manufacturing environment, we may see a full time HR person brought in earlier to support employees who need help with the technology required for timekeeping and benefit enrollment. Employees in this environment might require more detailed communication through face-to-face meetings. On the flip side, you may have a virtual workforce that moves throughout the country, autonomously servicing your client base. In that case, employees can be provided online tools so HR needs will be reduced. Other factors that impact the decision to include a dedicated human resources function are a high amount of turnover, extensive training, recruiting and retaining top talent, and a higher number of employees for whom English is a second language.

What we suggest is that you are forward thinking and consider whether now is the right time to look at these issues for your business, employees, and clients. There are many ways to address the HR needs, and likely you can differentiate yourself by using some method of professional human resources that may not be obvious to the others in the industry.

Ways to incorporate Human Resources within the organization

Once you have determined that HR needs a greater or redefined focus in your organization, you have a number of options for establishing your human resources function. The options range from providing a full time HR resource to adding a solution with more limited availability to the organization. There are outsourcing options that may also be appropriate based on the needs of your team. Managers must weigh the pros and cons of each option when making the decision that is appropriate for their organization. Consider factors such as access to your management team, employee response time, and strategic needs of HR.

As with all business decisions, you must evaluate the triangle of cost, quality, and speed. Business classes continue to teach the important trade off of all three components in any part of business. It is unlikely to have anything that is low cost, high quality, and done extremely quickly. Human Resources activities are no different. As you evaluate the options for HR below, consider which of these is most critical.

- Is HR an area you can afford to add as a stand-alone department?
- What is the tolerance for adequate programs as opposed to those that may be best in class?

Should manager and employee issues be answered immediately, or is there an acceptable window for reply?

Considering each of these questions with honest reflection on the culture of your business will help drive the right decision. Consider where are you willing to be flexible and what are the needs your team cannot live without. This will help you find the solution that is right for your team.

Consider our **FIPE** tool to evaluate the possible arrangements in adding HR to your team.

Full-time – Hiring a full-time resource should be considered for businesses that employ more than 70 employees or those that have administrative needs taxing the current structure of the organization. While 70 employees do not meet the benchmark for a full time professional, it is important to start to consider HR as a more formal function at this size. Full-time HR can also be an effective solution in growth organizations or those with exceptional recruiting or training needs. A company that chooses to add this type of HR function to its structure needs to ensure that their budget is being wisely spent. The management team must expect that the new HR leader will offer fresh ideas that enhance current initiatives.

It is incumbent upon current leadership to be open to a new voice. It's not helpful to create a situation in which new ideas of operation are turned down or when current staff is unwilling to hand over HR responsibilities.

If your strategic plan calls for expansion, you may want a more integrated HR partner on the leadership team. This will allow for communication of your message to the team and an attention to details of the growth plan to ensure the right talent is in the right seat. If you are able to meet your strategic goals with a small team of employees, this may be the perfect time to bring in an HR professional on a contract basis.

Internal – Offering the position to a current employee can be an excellent growth opportunity for a successful team member. The HR position might be offered as a way to develop and add new skills for high performing talent. Selecting a valued member of the team and providing growth and training sends a positive message to the rest of the employees. If co-workers respect the person being moved into the HR role, they will know that management values HR, and appreciates high quality work in current positions. Resist the temptation of moving a poor worker to an administrative role in the HR function.

An internal HR resource requires a base salary, benefit package, and a bonus if offered to other professional team members. There is also the impact on statutory benefits of unemployment, workers compensation, and Social Security that must be considered. However, when considering the line items of your budget such as labor cost, benefit expenses, compliance etc., there should be a realization that the cost of a professional HR focus can be offset by long term savings. In addition, the expense of HR will be offset by the ability of your management team to focus time and energy on their areas of expertise.

Part-Time – This is an option open to smaller employers, generally those that have fewer than 50 employees. At this size, a dedicated HR professional will struggle to fill 40 hours of impactful work. Part-time HR professionals also work well in organizations that are geographically dispersed with larger employee populations. Employees in remote offices do not expect an immediate reply as they are generally dealing with corporate via phone and email.

Having a dedicated part-time HR team member will generally provide the organization 10 – 25 hours per week of HR support. Your HR function will be tied to the goals and strategies of the operation, bond with employees, and provide the flexibility to ebb and flow as your budget and HR function evolves. This HR team member should be as skilled and professional as a full-time counterpart.

External - There are a number of options available to incorporate HR resources utilizing the services of external professionals. Even if you have internal resources, you will find that parts of your human resources puzzle are outsourced. Virtually all organizations outsource the management of their payroll, retirement, and health insurance plans for example. This is an efficient way to utilize talent for the expertise and eliminate the need for your HR resource to be an expert in every aspect of the employee relationship.

An external solution can be useful in an organization that is focused on high growth requiring extensive recruiting as well as those where it is essential for managers to remain focused on critical business functions. The external solution is also useful in organizations where the reliance on top talent is not a strategic component. In these cases, external groups with a focus on customer service-oriented may serve employees well.

Most organizations utilize payroll processing firms that help with unemployment, tax filing, and compliance reporting as an external resource. If desired, there are ways to outsource the entire function of human resources. The most popular options in this scenario include independent consultants, consulting groups, Professional Employer Organizations (PEO) and

FIPE for success...

An on-line advertising company was formed in 2007. There was no need for strategic HR, and they elected to outsource the HR function. They were growing rapidly and helping employees with company specific issues was important.

A bright, eager receptionist was promoted and become responsible for maintaining employee files, answering employees' questions and other HR tasks. She utilized the PEO for issues requiring a higher level of HR knowledge and complexity.

They anticipated being at 325 employees within the year. They added a Vice-President of HR. The VP was part of the executive management team and reported to the CEO.

The VP and CEO agreed to bring HR in house and eliminate the need for the PEO.

Within five months, the organization added four people to the HR team. This group then hired eighty-five new employees in three months. They relied on HR consulting to transition current employees from the PEO to the internal operation. Once the transition was complete, the new HR department was successful at maintaining the ongoing operations.

Administrative Services Organizations (ASO).

Many organizations will find a solution in one of the FIPE arrangements. We see equally as many who find the right solution for their organization is a combination of these solutions. As we have stated, almost all organizations use external resources for part of the HR function. There are also many times where a combination of full and part-time works well to have both administrative and strategic support. As you would with any analysis, consider all options and allow for a combination that will meet the needs of your team.

The impact of HR in dispersed workforces

It is common for organizations to operate multiple facilities, have team members working from home, and manage completely virtual workforces. Non-traditional workforces tend to work well with the spectrum of HR options we have outlined. For these groups, it may be less important to have someone sitting in the corporate office 40 hours a week in exchange for being supported through technology or self-service options.

In the case of multiple facilities, we find that employees are comfortable working with an administrative team member at their location. In these cases, adding HR to the home office may be a burden for everyone. Virtual workforces are generally comfortable finding answers for themselves and waiting for an email reply to an inquiry that would delay your adding a dedicated HR resource to meet employee needs. Consider, though, that employees who don't work out of the corporate office can feel disconnected and unappreciated. HR can be an invaluable resource to provide communication and connection to your mission and goals for those working outside the corporate offices.

Reporting relationship of human resources within the organization

Whether an internal or external function, where the human resources function reports within the organization will impact how HR is viewed. If HR administration and oversight is given to a clerical team member with other responsibilities, the team will view internal employee issues as an administrative function rather than a valued resource. If HR reports to a leadership team member who's a valued decision maker, the message is given that HR is critical to your organization. In the best case, the team member responsible for human resources will be included in executive meetings and seen as a driving force for the organization. Leadership connection demonstrates a focus on incorporating employees into the planning of business initiatives.

When possible, HR should have a direct line to the President or CEO of the organization. The direct reporting relationship allows HR to have a primary focus on supporting organizational initiatives through employees. HR should have first hand knowledge of the strategic plan, and responsibility for meeting the goals that intersect with employee behaviors. Where it is not realistic for your HR administrator to report directly to the CEO, the CEO should have direct contact with the HR team member or resource on a regular basis. These critical one-on-one meetings will provide essential business knowledge for the HR team and help the CEO keep their finger on the pulse of employee activity.

Let's look at various scenarios of reporting and analyze how each might impact the organization:

> **HR reporting directly to the President/CEO** – One of the most valuable pieces of this relationship is that it allows for HR to be the conduit from the CEO to the employees, as well as from the employees to the CEO. This requires the HR person to focus on what is really driving the business and how the employee population can help make this happen. The HR function in this structure has the primary goal of operational alignment in their problem solving and decision making initiatives.
>
> A critical piece of this relationship is to have an HR person who is skilled at

filtering and positioning messages in both directions. Your HR leader must listen to employee issues. They are then expected to consider the content and share issues that drive the organization with the top executives, considering that the mangers have limited time. Your HR leader must be a gatekeeper for the executives in identifying issues of importance and bringing those forward. For this relationship to be effective, the HR representative must be given the authority to solve issues at lower levels in the organization quickly and effectively.

Where the reporting relationship is direct to leadership, the person responsible for HR will generally have the title of Director of Administration, Director of Human Resources, or Office Manager.

HR functioning within the finance department

– In most situations, your CFO or controller is not interested in human resources. Even where there is an interest in HR, there are other priorities that are critical to business initiatives that need their attention. However, it is common that human resources

> **It's just too much...**
>
> A small accounting firm had 30 employees. The finance manager was responsible for HR. She had taken classes and attended meetings to try and learn the HR function.
>
> Recruiting accounting professionals was very difficult, and while it did not take a great deal of time, it caused extreme frustration. Larger firms were drawing top talent away. During benefit enrollment her time was completely taken up by meetings and enrollment.
>
> The managing director asked that she re-write the employee handbook before the first of the year. That was the last straw!
>
> She asked...which would you like – the handbook or year-end financials? The solution - hire an HR generalist to take on the employee issues critical to the firm. She managed the generalist and kept everyone happy!

administration sits within the finance function. This is likely due to the fact that payroll and benefit activities are closely aligned with the finances. When HR is part of the finance team, it tends to be more administrative – meaning it's not part of strategic planning or advancing business goals. The focus is based on cutting costs and limiting the customer service component of the HR relationship.

In this structure, the management team does not receive much human resources expertise or support. While there may be a direct report to your finance executive with some human resources knowledge, they will typically have shared responsibility of accounts payable, receivables, or payroll.

As we mentioned earlier, it's often the CFO or controller who – sometimes reluctantly - is the person responsible for human resources activities. It is common that a CFO will attend HR conferences and training to gain knowledge and ensure compliance. But it may be at the expense of collecting past due invoices or preparing the quarterly reports for a timely filing with your bank. This is a lost opportunity cost that must be included in evaluating the human resources impact on the organization. If this is the situation in your operation, consider whether an HR administrator would free up time to focus on what is critical to drive the business and save resources.

A dedicated HR professional who reports to a CFO can have an effective relationship if the CFO values the ability of HR to drive strategic initiatives. Your HR team member should be seen as a professional who can meet with employees, solve problems, and has a good working relationship with senior management. Where these competencies and relationships exist, reporting to a CFO who is a partner in employee engagement can be very successful.

The HR professional who reports within the finance unit will typically have the title of HR Generalist or HR Administrator.

HR responsibilities aligned with other or multiple departments – In some organizations there is a decentralized structure for HR. In these structures, each functional or regional area may have its own people responsible for pieces of the HR puzzle. For example, managers may be responsible for their own recruiting, new hire orientation and performance management. They retain employee files and answer questions from the public relating to employee information.

This often sends the message throughout the organization that employees are not a resource to be managed on a strategic level. It is difficult to gain a clear understanding of employee needs, and the organization may be providing training and benefits that are not relevant to the overall employee population. Where HR is parceled out to various people, there is a lack of alignment between employees and the strategic initiatives of the business. Various departments may duplicate initiatives, and opportunities for advancement may not be presented across the full organization. We cannot advocate this strategy for most organizations.

In decentralized HR operations, the primary area of concern beyond redundancies, missed opportunities and impact on strategy are issues associated with compliance. Managers may be capable of hiring and firing, but have little understanding of HR compliance. This will open the business up to complaints of discrimination with the Equal Employment Opportunity Commission and other regulatory agencies. Employees with questions or issues on payroll practices may feel they have nowhere to turn for advice, and choose to seek clarification with the Department of Labor. Top talent may find it easier to go to a competitor demonstrating a focus on employee engagement rather than stay with a disconnected team.

If parceling out HR responsibilities to various departments does occur, it requires disciplined cooperation among managers and a watchful eye by executives. It can be more difficult to manage the higher-level aspects of human resources such as strategic alignment, compliance, or employee engagement. HR at the local or department level should be considered an administrative solution to human resources.

Wherever HR sits, it is critical that HR be aligned with the leadership team. With the knowledge of strengths, weaknesses, opportunities, and threats the organization anticipates being able to face, HR will be a valuable member of the decision-making team. This information and basis for leadership will also allow HR to be seen as a trusted resource for your employees. If HR is left out of these crucial conversations, employees will not have the confidence that employees are of critical importance to leaders.

Qualities to look for in an HR professional

Learning the administrative tasks of HR is not the hard part. Finding talent that is able to embrace the soft skill of being able to work with the line workers and executives at the same time is a critical skill. Whichever part of **FIPE** you choose, the same skills for the individual that is tasked with HR responsibility are necessary. Your future HR leader needs to possess exceptional communication skills in order to present initiatives to the management team. At the same time, there is a critical need to communicate with team members, some of who may have minimal literacy skills. Complex points will need to be explained to employees at all levels such as how a high-deductible health plan works or changes to employee self service sites.

Literature on HR leadership consistently highlights the following competencies among high achieving HR teams:

- Trusted advisor – able to coach and guide the leadership team in various situations that impact employee interaction

- Executive – participate as member of the team driving business forward

- Business knowledge - posses knowledge of the

entire business including budget, technology, finance, sales and operations

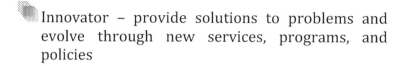Innovator – provide solutions to problems and evolve through new services, programs, and policies

Vendor Manager – ability to set expectations, evaluate performance, negotiate terms, and engage services

If you are relying on external resources, the same skill set is essential to support your team.

Attention to detail should be balanced against the knowledge of which compliance activities have to be closely followed and which can be monitored from the sideline. Take into account self-confidence and the ability to multi-task. And of great importance, you need to be able to see this person as part of the upper echelons of leadership within the organization. HR is the role that will be the face of the management team to employees. HR is the conduit between high-level decision-making and implementation at the employee level. Therefore, it is critical that you have a team member that will align with your business goals and portray a positive image of the management team at all times.

Deciding who to move into HR

This decision will be based on the availability of internal talent and the skill set of those interested in the role. The selected team member must be one that is trusted throughout the organization and has the ability to balance the requirements of compliance with the need to run your business. The HR resource must understand the administrative pieces that come with human resources responsibility, but also interested in elevating their current skill set to one that ensures your organization is up to date on the latest compliance obligations.

Discuss the desire to formalize HR with a few internal team members. Generally we find there is interest from office managers, administrative assistants, or others that are involved in processing of HR data today. HR allows these employees to retain and embrace their skill set while taking on a more visible role in the organization. Many employees in administrative functions have become more efficient in their primary role through the use of technology freeing up a portion of their workday. This may create an opportunity to take on a more comprehensive position integrating employees and the business operation.

My CFO/Controller is fine at handling the HR function

There are professionals in the accounting function that enjoy the diversity of responsibility that make up the human resources function. For these team members your accounting department is quite capable of handling the HR function. Who is concerned if you leave HR with accounting? You might want to check with your CFO or controller. Accounting is often stuck with HR administration and the only correlation between the two is the insurance and payroll functions.

The skills of a successful accountant are extremely different from that of a successful HR leader. The time and patience required to coach employees and managers is generally not where finance team members excel. The precise analysis of accounting transactions is an activity that would send most HR people to another department. The accounting department is often capable of getting the HR job done, but they will likely complete the pieces that are required and not add value beyond that.

Consider the time HR administration takes away from critical finance functions. Your CFO may be spending time entering hours into the payroll system when negotiations could bring a better interest rate by interviewing multiple banks. If you have a controller who adds value by managing the relationship with the bank and watching the budget for opportunities and threats, they can add value beyond the HR function. Consider the opportunity cost of having accounting focused on HR activities, and what value can be added if you bring in a skilled HR professional.

We have seen more than one excellent controller or CFO leave a position because they are the only option for human resources services. If a professional's career focus is to be a great accountant with financial responsibility, HR is often not where their passion lies. Is your accounting leader complaining about HR or using HR activities as an excuse for missed deadlines? Listen before it's too late and they walk out the door for a dedicated accounting position at your competition.

Part-time employees have other obligations and won't focus on my business

Consider someone who can devote a minimum of eight to 20 hours per week, depending on your needs. While it may take your current administrator five hours to complete an activity in HR, your part-time professional will not take that long. You will be hiring someone that knows and understands the field and should be able to handle the same task in an hour or two.

HR is still a field dominated by women and part-time work will often provide an opportunity for a win-win situation. There is generally a pool of candidates (men and women alike!) who have elected to leave the workforce to raise a family, but would love to use and retain their professional skills. Providing an opportunity to work 9 am to 2 pm will allow those that have chosen to leave the traditional workforce a way to retain their professional position and raise their children at the same time. There are also a number of semi-retired employees who are not ready to spend their day on the golf course or watching soap operas, but don't want to work 50 hours a week either. Creating a schedule where your team member would work a portion of each day four to five days a week can be a win-win for both parties.

There should be an agreement that the HR resource is available to management at times they are not in the office. As a business, you will accept that a parent won't be in the office on school holidays and a once-retired team member may have more travel planned than your typical vacation would allow. However, they will be willing to work off hours if needed to get the job done, and be available to you at busy times such as open enrollment for benefits or if you have a high recruiting month.

Budgetary concern is often a key component to deciding to move to a part time resource. Your budget may only allow for an administrative salary, but your needs may be more strategic in nature. Identify an employee looking to trade the long hours and pressure of a full time position with a more flexible environment and salary you can work with.

Department managers like to be in control

HR should be providing advice and taking tasks off the management team so they can focus on where their expertise lies. What HR should not be doing is keeping managers from making the decisions necessary to run the day-to-day operations. Managers should still retain control of the decisions that impact their production.

Bringing HR into your business

In small organizations, managers are generally responsible for their own HR activities such as recruiting, training, performance management, and compensation planning. They don't have the time or skill to effectively manage these functions. For example, top candidates may lose interest in your operation because the recruiting process is chaotic and they have a difficult time getting answers.

Managers often neglect conducting annual performance reviews. This creates situations where employees aren't given feedback or the ability to discuss future opportunities within the organization. Employees view this as impeding their professional progress and a lack of concern for their well-being. At some point, managers' lack of attention will reduce employee engagement to your business.

On the flip side, you may find managers are running off to training sessions on HR topics so they have the skills they need to complete this portion of their responsibility. Typically this is not a good use of their time or your money. Your managers may be utilizing other professionals to get answers to HR questions that could be easily answered by an in-house resource. It will likely take a manager many hours to find an answer to a question that an HR professional could answer immediately, or would have solved before the manager ever had to get involved.

Typically, you'll hear from the management team that the human resources responsibilities are hindering their ability to meet the goals of their position. The majority of non-HR managers do what they have to do in HR to get the job done. They don't enjoy the HR piece of the job, but it's their responsibility. Managers aren't going to get excited about working with employees on benefit enrollment and answering government inquiries about how many people you hired last month.

Listen if your managers say, "I can't get to that because another employee needs something," or if your month-end financials are late because the CFO had three new hires this week. Tasks that interface with team members will generally come first – especially when the new hire is standing at the door asking how they are supposed to fill out direct deposit paperwork. This may be occurring at the detriment to the activities you need to run your business.

 Pose this question to your management team: What do you spend time on each day that is human resources related? What goals and initiatives do you have that aren't being addressed due to employee issues and administration? While speaking with them, keep in mind that bringing in HR may feel like they are giving up control. The key to the conversation is to understand what opportunities are being lost by having managers responsible for the HR function.

HR as a coach and sounding board

Human resources should be the internal coach working with your management team, implementing business initiatives, preparing current employees for succession and looking at ways to ensure the employees have the skills and resources they need to meet the demands of the future. HR should be exploring ways to develop key talent for the future, both internally and externally.

Generally, we find that HR spends a significant amount of time working with line managers and coaching them to improve employee efficiency. Providing a resource for

---

A simple solution...

A manufacturing employee was excellent at his job. However, he was consistently late to work. The manager tried everything and had given the employee a final warning of termination. HR knew that the employee was a top performer and had been identified to become a manager in the future.

HR met with the employee. He confided that the public transportation system was unreliable. The commuter system was more reliable but at $9 per hour he couldn't afford the monthly ticket.

HR devised a plan – for three months the company purchased the higher priced ticket. They agreed that if he were at work on time every day, the company would raise his salary enough to afford the ticket permanently. The employee was at work on time every day.

Within 18 months he was promoted to a plant manager role at a new facility in Nashville, Tennessee. This same employee went on to become a top executive in the company.

your management team that can develop employee improvement plans can turn employees with productivity issues into top performers. Save time by having HR enter the conversations early so employees understand what needs to change. There may be an underlying situation that is easily solved through coaching. Often HR will be the objective team member who can map out a long-term strategy, or help make the decision that the time has come to separate an employee from the organization.

Listening skills are essential

HR must be able to listen, evaluate, and share issues with the appropriate members of your team. Employees vent frustrations to the HR resource. Open discussions can be productive if the HR team member is able to properly coach the employees on next steps. Your HR resource will need to be respectful of the employee's concern, but get the employee back to work after having expressed the issue. You want the HR manager to have a good barometer and know what should be elevated to the management team, and what can be addressed without involving other managers. There will be a number of conversations where no action is required, in which your HR resource must listen, provide comfort, and move on.

Confidentiality is Key

HR is a balancing act of confidential information, not only for the employees but for decisions made by the executive team, too. For example, if an employee comes to discuss a harassment situation but asks that it be kept confidential, the HR manager must know there's a legal obligation to share the information with executives. There are appropriate ways to explain this to employees, and it should be done in a way that is respectful of their concerns. At the same time, HR will often be privy to confidential conversations and data within the management team that impacts business operations. For example, HR might be aware that due to sales a product line is soon to be eliminated, but can't provide this information to employees interested in promotion to that department. Confidentiality from the general employee population is critical if HR is to be involved in corporate decision-making. Keeping aspects of the organization confidential is a critical piece of the HR puzzle.

Often, managers make the decision to exclude HR from sensitive conversations. This could be at the detriment of long-term strategy: information regarding future business goals and operations are a critical component of all HR decision-making. Consider the HR resource that is charged with recruiting, but is not aware of an upcoming capital expenditure that will require new computer skills on the shop floor. Were HR aware of these planned initiatives, it could alter recruiting requirements to provide long-term success for the operation.

HR is filled with confidential information, and this is a critical component to the decision to place HR internally or externally to the organization. While it can be tempting to consider a preference toward an external solution based on confidentiality, a significant amount of data relating to employees is always maintained within your organization, stored in your information systems, and used by your finance department. Security of employee data is an expectation of the HR team, and a minor piece of the HR puzzle when managed properly.

Human Resources is the party-planning department

We spend more time with our co-workers than our families. Employees have no choice as to who is in the next cubical, or who the project team members are. But to be successful in your

A productive picnic...

A manufacturer in the mid-west held an annual company picnic for their 600 employees and family members. The picnic was held in the parking lot of the facility and family was invited to tour the factory and see where their loved one worked.

There was a round robin soccer tournament where each department competed against other departments. In the dunk tank sat an executive team member as the target. When lunch was ready, department managers assisted the HR department in serving lunch to the attendees and thanking them for a job well done.

The budget for the day was large, but the advantages gained by the business could be felt in the teamwork and respect throughout the year.

organization, they must get along, be productive, and hopefully excel. This comes from managing the relationships in the workforce, which can be enhanced through effective HR activities.

Organized activities can be a productive way for employees to take a break and form personal connections with their co-workers. The personal connections are critical when urgent client needs arise or there is a crisis on the production line. We have all seen examples where employees work to help their friends, and will sabotage the needs of a co-worker that they do not have a positive relationship with.

There should be events throughout the year that allow managers to thank an employee for a job well done. Important events are held for business updates to share information with employees and help them understand the direction the leaders have identified for the next quarter.

HR should be coordinating these events on both a small and large scale. The event or program should be aligned with the culture of your organization and always have a business purpose – even when that focus is on social interaction. Organizations do still have Secret Santa exchanges, birthday celebrations, and employee picnics. The focus of your HR department must be to conduct these activities with communication and team-building goals that serve the business needs.

In general, the scale of events is more limited than they were in the past. This is due to budget restrictions as well as a shift in the HR leaders business focus toward activities tied to the company mission or strategic goals.

Action Items for how HR will look in your organization:

1. Review the current HR administration with your leadership team

2. Get input from trusted advisors –can benefit from a dedicated HR resource

3. Review your budget for a reliance on HR activities

4. Create a list of HR responsibilities and determine the number of hours a week a skilled resource would need to meet your goals

5. Consider internal candidates that may be interested in taking on HR responsibilities

Chapter Four

Compliance

Businesses of all sizes have government regulations they must be aware of and comply with. This includes the smallest business with only one employee on a part-time basis. That employee is still entitled to proper pay and a work environment that is free of discrimination. Our survey of small businesses shows that once a business has determined how human resources will fit into their corporate structure, compliance is the second most important concern.

Human resources professionals consider compliance a major part of their duties. In businesses that do not have a formal HR function, compliance awareness should be assigned to a member of the management team. The organization must keep current with laws and understand which of those impacts the organization. There are deadlines throughout the year that stem from many of these laws and dictate when forms must be completed and where to report employment statistics. Typically, states, cities, counties, and other municipalities create additional regulations there are more stringent requirements that must be complied with as well. Organizations that operate facilities in multiple locations are required to comply with regulations specific to where employees work, which gets especially complicated when a business operates across state lines.

Add to that the fact that the vast majority of what HR considers when making decisions are not by-the-book regulations, but ever evolving legal precedence. The verdict in a particular lawsuit will guide HR professionals in the application of policies and procedures to ensure your organization will not end up with a similar legal action to that seen in a particular case. Since a business cannot control which employees will pursue legal action, at least HR professionals can learn from the example of others and protect the company when possible.

But don't be mistaken: while HR is responsible for awareness of and compliance with laws, it shouldn't be the primary focus. Laws must be adhered to, but are also a springboard for critical business conversation. It is not productive to have an HR function that spends time using legal compliance as the excuse to keep you from meeting your strategic goals. There are many ways to simultaneously address business needs, remain compliant, and move initiatives forward. Having a strategic HR partner is essential to ensure that your managers are receiving great counseling on legal obligations, as well as brainstorming solutions that meet the needs of the operation at the same time.

COMPLIANCE

Many business owners do not have complete awareness of full scope of employment law that impacts their organization. Consider this list of laws that typically impact every business:

- Section VII of Civil Rights Act
- American with Disability Act
- Family and Medical Leave Act
- Fair Labor Standards Act
- Immigration Reform and Control
- Federal Labor Relations Act/Board
- Occupational Safety and Health Administration

These are just the major laws HR deals with on a consistent basis. The complexity of managing the laws starts with an understanding of which laws impact your organization, what reporting requirements are involved, and how to apply each to your employees. This is only a brief outline of major laws and does not begin to touch on the laws that must be considered in the various subject areas. For those specialty areas that are given full chapters, we will outline laws that come into play as appropriate.

My HR functions is feels like the police

It's not the HR person's job to police the organization. Rather, HR should be creating policies and thinking like a management team member who is expected to make strategic decisions that align with your enterprise while keeping you compliant. If this isn't how your HR administrator takes action, the problem may be with the person, not the position. Within the company, it's HR's job to ensure that managers understand policies and directives, and the basis upon which they were created. A company should offer training to managers regarding legal obligations and the ways they've been enacted within the company in the past. Policies need to be enforced by the entire organization; this is a primary responsibility of management.

I trust my HR resource to ensure we're compliant

Trust, but Verify! This is an essential obligation of executives. You would never go a year without an audit of your accounting records – even if the original process began as a bank mandate. Owners sleep better knowing that an outside entity has reviewed the company's financial position and is confident that procedure and activities are in order. The human resource function has access to payroll and costly benefits, and could incur large fines and penalties if they are not complying with requirements. Why don't you have this function audited as well? Because most owners don't consider the high risk/reward equation in the HR function.

Getting a clear snapshot of where a business stands on compliance can be difficult. Your current CFO, office manager, or HR administrator is likely to tell you that you are compliant. This is a fair answer to the best of their ability, but there is also a reason you picked up this book. There's the fear of being on the wrong side of compliance in areas you aren't even aware of. When conducting an HR assessment, we often uncover areas of compliance that small business owners did not know existed.

In organizations that have fewer than 100 employees, it is typical to have someone without formal HR training managing the HR function. Organizations with fewer than 300 employees generally have a lean team that is responsible for all aspects of the human resources function. Where there is a dedicated HR manager or generalist, the employee is doing what is needed to meet the needs of the organization on a daily basis. While your HR professional is likely to be doing a good job, there are areas of compliance that are easy to miss. Best practices may be available that your sole practitioner has not come in contact with. A good audit of HR practices every three to five years will help verify the compliance issues and provide a great resource of best practices to your HR team.

Ultimately, compliance is the responsibility of the entire

management team and should be the concern of ownership. The fines levied by the Department of Labor, Equal Employment Opportunity Commission, Department of Homeland Security, Occupational Safety and Health Administration and the Internal Revenue Service can be staggering. The highest fines are those that are given to employers who act in a willful disregard for requirements. Those are the business owners, executives, and human resources professionals that were aware laws and protocols existed but did nothing to address the compliance requirements at their organization. In many cases, the fines for being unaware of laws that impact your employees and your organization compound on a daily basis. Conduct a review of your current compliance position in order to minimize the risk associated with a government audit.

After years of consulting and participating in many government conversations around compliance, we find that organizations demonstrating an honest attempt to meet their obligations are treated with respect and leniency. Companies that make no attempt to understand obligations – or worse, those that know the obligations and ignore them – are the organizations that receive crippling fines from government entities.

Conducting a Human Resources Audit is essential

The terms "audit" and "assessment" are often used interchangeably in the human resources and legal communities. It is critical for a business owner to understand what outcomes they should expect when moving forward with a review of human resources. An audit generally focuses on compliance and should return results that are specific to the organization. The deliverable should include tools that will allow internal team members to take the appropriate action to fix the issue identified. Similar to an accounting audit, they will look for best practices and ensure your record keeping is in order. An assessment is generally a broad review of the human resources function that will include review of your staffing model in human resources as well as alignment with the strategic goals of the organization. The assessment includes all areas discussed in an audit. For the purposes of this section we will use both terms to mean the overall review of your HR function.

The goal of the HR review should be to confirm compliance with all obligations of your organization relating to size, location, and industry.

There should be a component of the review that considers the employees handling HR today and how they may conduct their activities more efficiently or utilize current best practices. A good HR audit will provide high-level solutions to problems that can be addressed internally.

Evaluating the knowledge

Assessment as teamwork....

A provider of in-home healthcare had recently been spun off into its own operation. The HR Manager was the former HR assistant. She was able to retain talent and create processes for the new organization. She did not have formal HR training, but had a great mentor in the former organization.

After 18 months on her own, she knew her processes were OK, but not perfect. She reached out to her benefit broker and asked for HR assistance. The broker recommended a consultant that could complete an HR audit. The budget of $6,500 was approved.

The audit was conducted over three days in the office, and a few weeks of document review by the consultant off site. The deliverable was a report to the executive team about recommendations in Human Resources.

The final report indicated that compliance was good, but there were some opportunities for improvement. These included: I-9 review; anti-harassment training for the team; employee handbook updates; pay notification were among a few of the suggestions.

The HR Manager retained the consultant on an as needed basis going forward. They fixed the issues identified together, and worked together to remain compliant.

base of members of your current HR team as well as those you are considering moving into this area is a helpful component to an assessment. The creation of a good job description is a very effective way to ask the professional completing the assessment to determine if you have the right talent in human resources. They should create an analysis of skill deficiencies of your HR team based on the job description and provide resources for training that are readily available.

When interviewing professionals for an HR assessment, ask for examples of the type of recommendations they have made to clients similar in size and complexity to your organization. You should see ideas that are practical, goal-oriented and within a budget that makes sense for your operation. It will not be helpful to align yourself with a professional who feels an MBA or law degree is essential to move forward with an HR function. A resource that is aware of local training that can be completed quickly and cost effectively indicates an individual who understands your needs and will provide realistic solutions. Yes, PeopleSoft is one of the top human resource information systems on the market – but if you have 50 employees it won't make sense. An organization with a small team is best served using their payroll system as the database that manages employee information. Ensure your auditor makes recommendations that fit the small business environment.

You have a number of options when interviewing professionals to conduct the assessment. Labor attorneys and human resources consultants typically offer this service. You can also find resources by inquiring with your payroll and employee benefit vendors.

If you do choose to work with an employment attorney to conduct your assessment, ensure that they are a legal expert that spends the majority of time in employment matters. A general corporate attorney who advises you on employee issues may conduct the audit, but generally doesn't have the deep knowledge of human resources to give practical advice or solutions. A concern with engaging an attorney to conduct the assessment is a heavy focus on compliance and less expertise in the area of best practices. If compliance were your only goal, an employment attorney would be a valuable resource. Inquire if they can offer the service as part of an annual agreement or at a fee that is within your organization's budget.

HR consultants are an excellent resource for assessments. They provide the expertise in both compliance and best practices. You should look for a consultant that is certified as a Senior Professional in Human Resources (SPHR) and has many years of experience as an HR practitioner. The SPHR designation indicates that they have passed a stringent exam on the strategic and compliance components of the HR function, as well as meet the annual continuing education requirements for designation. Their deliverables should include a complete review of compliance as well as suggestions for best practices of your human resources function.

There are options to have the assessment conducted for free, or at a low cost. Understand that those entities that provide an assessment service at no charge are doing so with the possibility of uncovering future projects. While there is nothing wrong with this strategy, it should be discussed at the beginning of the project. You can also purchase an HR assessment from consultants and lawyers for a flat fee that may be less inclined to upsell future opportunities.

In either case, review past deliverables to clients and ensure the outcome you will receive is acceptable to you. While the "free" assessment may not generate an invoice, there will be a cost to your team in the time required to gather data for the audit and discuss findings. A list of reputable resources to conduct HR audits and assessments can often be secured from your accountant, attorney, local HR chapters, or other trusted advisors.

 If the expense of an external audit is a concern, the audit can be conducted internally. There are many books available on the subject, and HR Topics offers web based training opportunities to allow small organizations to complete the HR audit on their own. This can be found at hrtopics.com. If the decision is made to conduct the audit internally we recommend someone other than the person responsible for HR undertake the review. Consider a business acquaintance or trusted partner that has a small HR function – is it possible for your HR resources to trade auditing each another?

Staying on top of ever changing compliance requirements

An annual training budget for a team member charged with HR responsibility should be in the range of $1,500 to $3,000 annually. Depending on your location, a budget for travel may be required as well. This would allow the novice HR administrator to attend a number of entry level programs, and your more experienced HR professional to attend one or two annual conferences to stay on top of industry best practices. There are generally numerous programs conducted by employment law firms in your area at no charge that should be attended annually. If you choose to leave HR with a functional area, this budget is still appropriate. Your CFO or office manager will need to attend HR specific compliance training each year at a minimum.

Documentation requirements in human resources

Documentation is essential in the HR function, but has to be properly managed. When there is any dispute with an employee, the first thing reviewed is the written record.

Without documentation, a game of "he said, she said" develops and rarely does this resolve satisfactorily.

Law requires a great deal of documentation relating to the lifecycle of employees and the organization as an overall entity. Examples include completion of the I-9 form, OSHA 300 and 300A log, FMLA paperwork, COBRA forms, EEO-1 annual report, and many others documents that executives typically are not even aware of. The documentation requirements are an essential part of the HR Audit, and should be carefully reviewed by the professional you engage to handle this project for your team. The audit should ascertain whether up-to-date forms are being used and the documentation is accurately completed. Forms issued by government offices change often but are updated and available on the Internet.

There are many documents used within the HR function that are not required by law. However, if they are utilized in your organization the compliance impact should be considered. The forms in this category would include the employment application, performance review forms, written warnings, and other notes and documents kept relating to the employee and the workplace. A complete audit should include a review of these documents as well as those required by law.

Keeping records on employment decisions is a critical step in compliance. There should always be a formal record to indicate communication with employees has occurred around a given workplace incident. This will be used if there is a dispute with unemployment, a discrimination claim, or charge of wrongful termination.

At the same time, not every conversation has to have a formal notice signed by the employee put into a file. There are times when a verbal warning is appropriate, or a manager can make note of a conversation without the employee's signature. A skilled HR professional will understand what needs to be acknowledged by the employee and what can be retained at the company level.

It is critical to maintain documentation that is consistent among employees. In many employment disputes, the first thing courts or government entities review is how other similarly situated employees were treated. For this reason, we again encourage a central human resources function rather than each department manager being allowed to handle employment situations. The HR team member with responsibility can ensure that all employees have fair and similar treatment.

Employee file maintenance

All organizations should maintain official employee files. In the best case, these are maintained by a trusted member of your team and kept locked in a central location. In many cases there are documents that should be part of employee files retained in various areas of the organization. Finance keeps what they need related to payroll; the office manager retains portions related to emergency contact and key card access while the department manager has information concerning performance and training. Files that are strewn all over the organization can be difficult to assess, and will rarely meet the compliance obligations of the organization. Maintaining a central file system allows the organization to ensure that all pieces of the compliance puzzle are maintained.

Employee files may be maintained electronically. This provides a central storage and will typically attach to your payroll system for security and ease of retrieval. Virtual files are acceptable under most compliance requirements, and an excellent use of technology. With proper security, the virtual files will enhance productivity and accessibility of employee information by your management team.

Throughout the employment relationship, employees ask for a copy of their employee file. This is sometimes in response to an issue with their manager, or just the need to access information they did not retain a copy of in their files. Regardless of the employee's intention, all contents of the file must be provided to employees upon written request. It is not necessary that an employee receive a copy of the file immediately. It is recommended that when an employee does request a copy of a file you take time to review the contents and ensure the file is complete.

Laws dictating how employee files must be made available vary among states. There are generally provisions within the law to charge the employee for the copies made, including the labor required to comply with the request. It is essential that you check with current state law in the municipality in which the employee works to ensure compliance.

Employee handbook – to have or not to have

Policies can both help and hinder an organization. Once policies are documented, the organization will be obligated to follow the procedures outlined and benefits offered. Some owners feel that having an employee handbook will take away their flexibility to make changes for the organization. This is not really the case.

A well-written employee handbook is a roadmap that provides your team with guidelines by which to operate. It ensures that all department managers treat their employees the same way, and gives confidence to leadership that the culture of the organization is being maintained through policy.

In the absence of formal policy, employees will view actions taken by management as internal precedence and will assume they are entitled to the same treatment they believe was given to a co-worker. Without formal policy, an organization cannot point to the reason an employee was disciplined or terminated during a dispute. Employees without a handbook are more likely to take a supervisor's comment out of context, and insist they were promised a benefit when none is actually available.

An employee handbook also provides the manager with a document to refer to when denying an employee's specific request. Managers are often faced with situations where a top performer wants to take "just one more day off" and they can't see

> ### *Check the handbook please....*
>
> A small medical practice had nine employees. Two practicing physicians had the same team of three nurses, an office manager, and a receptionist for twelve years. The practice grew and they added a nurse and an administrative assistant.
>
> The team always knew how decisions were made, how much time off they got, pay policy etc. As they added new people, and the personal lives of the long-term employees changed, so did the work habits. The office manager came to the doctors and said they needed to start getting involved in performance management issues.
>
> The doctors just wanted to practice medicine. The decision was made to create an employee handbook defining the role of office manager as the leader of all staff. Authority was spelled out to discipline and terminate if the policies were not followed.
>
> The handbook allowed new team members to understand the rules – and the long-term group to receive a message that they either play by the rules or would be terminated.

an end in sight for the behavior. Where a handbook exists, managers can point to the attendance policy as the guideline being used throughout the organization. Where no policy exists, the employee sees the managers as unreasonable, and productivity is likely to drop.

Create policies that leave enough flexibility for situational decision-making in the future. It is common to use terms such as "generally", "often," and "may" rather than more concrete terms such as "will", "always," and "required." There are situations that arise in the employment relationship that require rules to be evaluated for the particular circumstances. This should be the exception, but when consideration is given for a good business reason, it's certainly acceptable.

There are certain policies that are essential to every employee handbook. Among the most critical policies to include are:

- ※ At-will employment
- ※ Anti-harassment and discrimination
- ※ Computer systems and email use
- ※ Pay practices
- ※ Confidentiality of company property, medical information and employee data

We encourage employers with more than ten employees to have an employee handbook. However, as seen in the medical office scenario there is no magic number. If your organization is small but would benefit from formal statement of policy and procedure, move ahead with a handbook. Often there are established norms that are poorly communicated to a new team member joining such a small group. With a handbook in place, management can be confident that all information is communicated as desired, while for current employees the handbook reinforces operational standards and provides a template for growth that all can follow. For organizations of any size, the handbook makes certain that decisions made regarding employees' questions and requests are based on objective criteria. Once created, an attorney or HR consultant skilled in handbook development should review the handbook.

The internal leadership team should review the handbook to be certain that the policies stated are properly reflected in the handbook. The handbook should be reviewed annually to ensure consistency and an accurate reflection of current policy and process. It is easier to change and adapt your handbook as you expand, rather than start a handbook when you have 50 employees and multiple operating rules within various departments.

The employee handbook is an excellent way to share the numerous communications that are required by the government. This may include FMLA requirements, pay practices and discrepancies, and the ability of the organization to view all email. While there are times the handbook can be used against an organization, the advantages of clear, writing guidelines for employee behavior and policy far outweigh the concerns

Action Items for compliance in your organization:

1. Conduct an assessment of your human resources function

2. Allocate a training budget to ensure HR remains up to date on federal, state and local law

3. Train managers on compliance obligations relevant to your organization

4. Write or review the current employee handbook

Chapter Five

Recruiting and retaining top talent

Recruiting top talent is an important issue for small business owners as it's critical to the success of any operation. The full process of recruiting is time consuming and can be fraught with errors. Organizations that do not possess a full-time HR resource find that the time required to identify and engage a new team member can be overwhelming. Compare that with a business that has a single team member responsible for the HR function: juggling phone screens, interviews and reference checks can take time away from other critical HR functions.

Smaller employers often consider themselves at a disadvantage when competing with large corporations for top talent for fear that their organization may not be well-known in the industry, and the benefit package is not as robust. Add to that the fact that there is a limited online presence to find the passive job seeker, and HR professionals may not be skilled at harvesting candidates from the Internet.

e best recruiting strategy any organization can have is
retain top talent and minimize unplanned turnover.
Having a goal of low turnover is not always a valuable
metric. Rather, establish a long-term plan that will
ensure your top talent is retained and those that are not
adding value are eliminated. Planned turnover is an
excellent way to provide current team members with
new opportunities. It also has the advantage of sending
the message that sub-standard performance is not
tolerated on your team.

Recruiting is a process of activities that must be managed
at every step. The chart below shows the required steps
in an effective recruiting program.

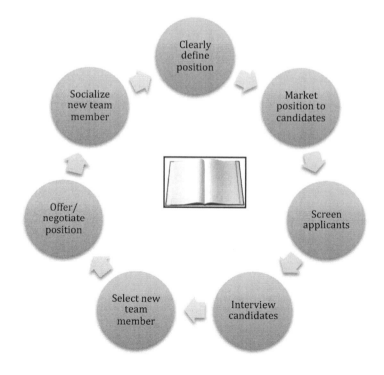

If you're new to recruiting or looking to maximize growth, consider attending a class to gain expertise on the recruiting cycle. Classes on the topic can range from a day to many weeks. Programs can be found at community colleges or through one-day training programs that provide basic and useful information on the best practices of staffing. If your organization requires the addition of more than three or four new employees annually, we recommend your HR professional or team  member assigned to recruiting participate in a training class on staffing and selection. Local resources for training are generally found on the Internet and offered on a regular basis.

Compliance issues faced when recruiting

There are a number of laws that impact the recruiting cycle to be aware of. The areas outlined below are very high-level indicators of recruiting compliance.

- Marketing the position – be aware of the wording used in ads. You cannot use words that would discriminate or deter a candidate from applying based on any criteria in Title VII, or other segments of the population that may be protected by law. Some examples of protected categories include age, gender, religion, etc.

- Interview Questions – all questions must be job-related and unbiased. You must ask similar questions of all candidates. Due to the complexity, we recommend all managers in the interview process have training on the legal guidelines of acceptable interview questions.

Americans With Disabilities Act – applies to candidates as well as employees. Interview space must be accessible to those with disabilities; and candidates can only be asked if they can complete the essential functions of the job with or without accommodation. These are just a few of the extensive requirements.

Citizenship – A candidate cannot be asked about their citizenship, only their ability to legally work in the United States. An I-9 form cannot be completed until after an employee has been offered a position. Once hired, the I-9 must be completed within 72 hours of starting work.

Background and credit checks – In general, there must be a job related basis for conducting background or credit checks. There are a number of state laws that govern this area; be sure to check before completing any investigation.

Pre-employment testing – concerns exist with tests' reliability and accuracy in predicting success of a candidate. For this reason, you should always use tests that are professionally marketed and compliant.

Medical exam – candidates cannot be subject to any medical testing, including a drug test, until the job is offered.

Someone quit; we need to hire another person quickly

Not so fast! Often a departing team member gives management a great opportunity to step back and evaluate. When a team member leaves, evaluate the workload of other employees; the impact technology may have on the position, and the possibility of outsourcing. Take the time to assess the position and the needs of the organization to determine what the next step should be.

Expect your management team to go through a similar evaluation process before any recruiting activities begin. Review and update the job description to ensure there is understanding at all levels of the organization as to the requirements needed from successful candidates. Analyze the criteria used in the past and consider if this is still applicable, taking into account aspects such as new skills required, use of technology, and interaction with customers.

Compensation requirements in the market may have changed as well. If the departing employee was with your organization for a number of years, their salary may be reflective of annual increases or acquired cross-training. The current salary may not be reflective of current market compensation, especially if you will be changing the requirements based on analysis. There may also be a drought of certain skills in the job market that are pushing up salaries of certain positions beyond the current rate of compensation. This is further discussed in chapter five.

Newspaper, Job Board, Employment Office, Social Media...Oh MY!

Whether you are looking for an employee or a contractor, there are many places to find qualified candidates. The placement of your marketing efforts should be specific to the industry, position, and other criteria that define the ideal candidate. For instance, you would not advertise for a new CFO the same way you would look for a manufacturing employee. In some cases you want to reach those not actively in the job market, while other times you need someone who can start quickly without needing to give notice. Have a clear understanding of the parameters of the candidate pool to select the appropriate location for your job announcement.

When looking for a professional or managerial candidate, word of mouth and networking is an excellent place to start. Your perfect hire might not be on LinkedIn or Twitter, but a friend or family member might let them know the position is available. Announce the position to your trusted advisors and networking community as a first step.

The most common formal recruiting today is done through social media and the Internet. The most popular job posting sites are LinkedIn, Monster, and Career Builder. Craigslist can also be a good source of candidates for hourly and entry-level positions. The key to managing the online community is having an application process that will not overwhelm the HR administrator or hiring manager. When possible, set up a dedicated email address for job inquiries. If recruiting is a regular part of your operation, consider an applicant tracking system. Affordable, basic systems are available from many payroll service vendors and will integrate with their systems for reporting. You can also purchase stand-alone software or utilize the functionality from the major job boards.

Newspapers are only viable today for very specific positions. While some managers feel there is an issue with accessibility to Internet recruiting by entry level talent, nearly all applicants have access to computers. The unemployment offices make computers and the Internet available, as do public libraries. Newspaper advertising should only be used as a way to notify the public of a job fair, or in cases where a specific audience is being targeted for their unique skill set.

Finding part-time employees

Methods discussed above apply to part-time employee recruiting as well. However, part-time candidates have left the traditional workforce and often are not actively searching for work. We find that word-of-mouth and Craigslist are especially effective in identifying a part-time candidate pool. Advertising the opening to the local school associations, religious organizations, and social service groups are all very effective in getting the word out about a part time position. When they are aware of a position that will work within their other obligations, they are energized by the opportunity.

One key to finding a great part-time employee is being flexible. When establishing a part-time role, the relationship between the organization and the part-time employees should focus on a commitment to the business and an agreement to meet the agreed upon deliverables. Openness to alternative arrangements and work schedules will allow you to add the talent of professionals who can meet your needs.

Evaluating résumés for a successful fit

With reliance on electronic advertising for positions, it is expected that all candidates have an résumé that can be submitted via the Internet. On initial review, the résumé should be error-free and organized. These are the two common traits we expect of all applicants, regardless of the position for which they're being considered. If candidates are willing to submit an résumé with spelling mistakes, imagine the quality of their work when they secure a position. While an résumé should exist for all, understand that for the entry level or hourly positions the résumé might be very basic. Some candidates have access to resources of expertise that are not available to others, and this should not be used to differentiate one candidate from another.

The résumé should be reflective of the skill set applicable to the position. While you can teach most skills, it is helpful to see an résumé that reflects advancement in an organization. Job hoppers were once defined as individuals who moved from one company to the next every four to six years. Today, it is common to find employees moving to a new organization after only two or three years. There are a number of reasons this may occur, and the reality should not automatically eliminate any candidate. Discussion regarding the movements will occur once you have a conversation with the candidate and determine whether the changes were made for a logical reason.

When it comes to a candidate's educational background, evaluate it honestly against skills the position requires. Managers tend to prefer college graduates for professional positions, giving little credit to those with extensive years of experience and no degree. The proliferation of online universities makes evaluating

ate programs more difficult. It is important for
ers to keep in mind that not all high school
ts have the opportunity to take the traditional path
to a four-year university immediately following high
school. Where a candidate has selected online education
as their means of securing a degree, give close evaluation
to the impetus for that choice. Add an analysis of the
experience the candidate brings to the work environment
before making a judgment.

Retaining top talent

The task of retaining top talent should be the
responsibility of all management team members. When
considering a plan for retention, identify your top talent.
These are the people who have the work ethic and
institutional knowledge that would put your organization
at a disadvantage if you lost them.
Employees who fit into the top talent
category are not necessarily the people
who have been around the longest, or
have a relationship with the customer you think you can't
live without. Top talent are the people you want on your
team in twenty years and you are therefore willing to
invest the time and resources to get them where they
need to be.

You don't want a situation in which you spend three
years training an engineer, only to have them go to the
competition because they offer better health insurance.

There are advantages to working with smaller operations, but they often have to be clearly outlined to employees. You may not be able to offer the same benefit plan, but you should have the ability to offer cross-training opportunities, participation in high-level decision-making, networking trips etc. These are the engagement activities that employees want to participate in and will keep them connected to your organization.

Your HR resource should be charged with the goal of ensuring your programs and packages are creative as well as competitive. Communication with employees should be an ongoing activity, and employee appreciation an everyday event. A small operation should be agile enough to show they can make changes to meet the needs of an individual employee. With HR in charge of these responsibilities, you should not only compete with the conglomerates in your industry but also excel at recruiting and retaining top talent.

Utilizing a professional recruiter

Professional recruiters, or headhunters as they are commonly referred to, can be a valuable asset to organizations. Recruiting is time-consuming and sometimes costly if not handled correctly. Compliance mistakes, lack of patience in identifying the right candidate, and the opportunity cost of managers spending time on the process all add to the cost incurred when recruiting is handled internally. Outsourcing the recruiting process can free up managers to focus on business initiatives and ensure the process is handled professionally and within compliance guidelines. Headhunters have access to large pools of candidates that they have met previously and can often be a valuable resource when a critical position is vacant unexpectedly.

Recruiters work with organizations in a number of ways. The most widely known is a contingency-based recruiting assignment. In this arrangement, the recruiter is not promised a fee unless they present a candidate that is selected by the company. The fee is higher than with other outsourced relationships, but if they are not successful in finding the ideal candidate there is no cost to the organization.

Replace the entire department – NOW!

A company of 100 employees moved their headquarters cross-country. The IT manager was not identified as a top performer, and only one member of the IT staff was interested in the new location. A total of 5 IT team members were needed in the new office.

The HR team knew this would be a time consuming project. Depth of knowledge of IT was critical. HR decided it would be best to secure the resources of a headhunter that was familiar with the IT positions as well as local talent.

After interviewing three vendors, they selected a partner that would work closely with HR to ensure candidates were strategically aligned with the vision of the organization and would allow some administrative tasks to be handled internally to keep costs down.

Within 6 weeks, a full IT team was hired, from the vice-president to an entry-level data entry clerk. All team members started as a group and the project come in within the budget approved by the executive team.

Many organizations like this situation because they can engage three or four different firms to work on the same search. This will ensure a wide pool of candidates and recruiters that are working quickly to find the best candidate for your organization.

Another common relationship is the retained or hourly search. In these agreements, the recruiter is paid a fee to find a candidate matching the requirements of the company and position. Retained recruiters generally spend more time getting to know the business and the culture of the team. The same recruiter is often utilized repeatedly and acquires a deep understanding of which candidates will be a good fit for the organization. Since there is no commission to focus on, the headhunter performs as a consultant and tends to be more selective in whom they recommend for the position. Retained search firms are generally in partnership with the organization and strive to streamline the process by only presenting the best candidates. Their fees are lower overall than a headhunter, but an agreed upon fee will always be due regardless of success.

Finally, temp-to-perm arrangements should be considered for certain positions. This is an agreement with an outside employment agency to provide an employee for a given period of time where there is currently a vacancy. If the employee is suitable for the long-term position, an additional fee is due. If the employee is not acceptable, the organization can let the agency know and they will send another candidate. This is very effective with positions where the learning curve is low, but the need to fit into the culture of the organization is high. Temp-to-perm arrangements are very popular in administrative assistant positions due to a relatively simple transferability of skills, and the time to assess a personality fit with the person being supported is valuable.

Action Items for recruiting in your organization:

1. Ensure job descriptions exist and reflect current requirements

2. Select applicable outlets and resources for marketing your positions

3. Train managers on the recruiting process

4. Identify top talent and create programs for retention

5. Consider outsourcing the recruiting function when appropriate

Chapter Six

Compensation and Benefits

Employers of all sizes battle with establishing a compensation program that is fair to employees and sustainable for the organization. There are many components of compensation that include base pay, annual increases, promotion increases, and bonuses. In a smaller business, these can be overwhelming to consider, and often it is the squeaky wheel that gets the increase in pay. Compliance in pay of workers is very complex, and where we see the most extensive complaints and fines from the Department of Labor.

Setting the proper rate for a starting salary is often based on inaccurate data, or deciding to meet the expectations of the candidate your managers are sure will be the perfect fit. Employees have come to expect annual salary increases; even where productivity has not improved and new skills have not been added. Employers are looking at salary increases as another expense to be absorbed rather than just raising prices annually. There has to be a systematic way for all businesses to evaluate pay and ensure that the total rewards provided to employees are aligned with the benefits the business receives from the employee's effort.

Benefit programs offered by a company are a combination of those mandated by the government and voluntary programs. An organization has the obligation to provide Social Security, Medicare, unemployment insurance, workers' compensation, and (within the next few years) health insurance. Employees also expect paid time off for vacations, illness, bereavement, jury duty, and a myriad of other activities that do not drive value to your bottom line. Many other benefits are typically provided that are not quantified but valuable to employees such as employee discounts on products, flexible work hours, and the ability to work from a remote location.

Total compensation is the compilation of all pay and benefits offered to employees. The focus of HR today is on total compensation, not simply the hourly or weekly salary offered to  employees. Employers should spend time reviewing typical compensation design programs and evaluate the competitiveness of their package. Industry associations generally provide comparable data for the industry, and there are numerous online resources that can be reviewed for common benefit packages.

Compliance obligations for compensation and benefits

The requirements of how organizations pay employees are extensive. The primary law governing pay is the Fair Labor Standards Act and it is essential that someone on your team become well versed in the requirements. Benefit law is also filled with obligations for the HR professional. There are many historical laws a business must be aware of when offering benefits, and the implementation of the Affordable Care Act, also knows as "Obamacare," adds to the complexity.

The key areas to consider in the compliance of compensation and benefit law are highlighted below.

Compensation-based compliance activities include:

- Fair Labor Standards Act – very complex law governing most aspects of pay from child labor to pay during travel. Ensure complete knowledge of all aspects of the requirements.
- Exempt employees – the definition of who is entitled to overtime and how that must be paid is very strict. Whether an employee is paid on a fixed salaried basis has no standing in compliance with the Fair Labor Standards Act. The only relevant point is whether or not an employee is subject to overtime.

89

- Independent contractors – this is the most basic definition of whether or not a worker is an employee. It is dictated by the Internal Revenue Service and not subject to the needs of the organization. If you utilize independent contractors on a regular basis, ensure you are up to date on the IRS requirements.
- Fair Pay Act – States that men and women must be paid similar rates for similar work.

Due to the complexity of compliance with the Fair Labor Standards Act, an HR assessment should include review of the payroll records. While it may seem odd to share such confidential data, a full assessment is only complete if they are able to review the hourly timesheets and actual pay as the Department of Labor would if you are audited.

Benefit-based compliance is changing quickly in 2014 – 2016. We list the common activities below, but encourage you to use Internet resources to ensure up-to-date compliance:

- HIPAA – enacted at the end of the twentieth century, HIPAA removed the pre-existing condition in most cases for group health benefit plans. The law also created extensive obligations regarding the privacy of an employee's health information as it related to the group health plan.

- ERISA – overall program that governs the communication of insurance plans with specific requirements and obligations relating to retirement planning.

- FMLA –If your organization has 50 or more employees within a 75-mile radius, this law will apply. It provides most employees up to twelve weeks of *unpaid* leave for medical conditions for themselves or immediate family members. FMLA was expanded recently to include situations relating to family members and military leave.

- COBRA –requires that you offer members of your health insurance plan the opportunity to remain on for a period of time after separation from the company depending on circumstance. This law applies to those with 20 or more employees, but there are various state laws that apply to smaller employers. Be aware of the requirements in your area if you had fewer than twenty employees in a six-month period.

- GINA –Businesses have recently become required to ensure the privacy of their employees as it relates to the use of any genetic information.

The Department of Labor, IRS, and EEOC are the agencies primarily responsible for the various laws impacting compensation and benefits. The penalties are extensive, and can be compounded if an organization is found to have knowingly ignored an obligation. Assigning one team member the responsibility for ongoing compliance with these laws is essential.

Annual performance review process

Providing employees feedback on their position and value to the organization is essential. Ongoing feedback and communication is a key function of management and should be occurring on a regular basis for all employees. Common thinking on the subject dictates that management conducts regular reviews no less often than once a year. This can be on an employee's anniversary with the organization, although some management teams find it easier to review all employees at the same time of year. This can be left to management preference, as long as the conversations occur.

Employees usually take the performance conference as an opportunity to discuss a raise in base salary and/or bonus. Best practice data show that the performance review is not the best time to review salary. This is because the natural inclination of employees is to focus on the desired salary change, and not the conversation surrounding goals and needs for improvement. In an ideal situation, the employee review would occur, and any appropriate change in pay would follow at a later date.

Making changes to an employee's pay

In the absence of a formal and competitive compensation program, retaining top talent can be very difficult. An organization must have their finger on the pulse of what the market is offering in terms of compensation for every position in the organization.

Complex market research is not typically necessary for the small business community. Your goal will be to look for information indicating average base salary for a position as well as any bonus or additional

> **Taking the pulse of the market...**
>
> A middle market leasing company paid employees industry average base salaries, but supplemented that with higher than average bonus payments based on annual profitability. Due to the difficult economy, base salaries were frozen in 2009 – 2011 while bonus payments remained stable. Employees had an expectation that salaries should increase annually. They were starting to leave for higher base salaries, even in cases where they knew the bonus potential was not as significant.
>
> The HR administrator recommended a salary survey. There was not an extensive budget for data. HR was able to secure a salary survey specific to the leasing industry in the geographic region for $495. They supplemented this data with a review of the self-reported information on salary.com – a popular survey site that employees use to compare their salary against others.
>
> These two data points showed employees were paid at the 85th percentile of the market. Approximately four positions were identified as those appropriate for an adjustment. The company created a memo for employees stating that the review occurred and most positions were paid at a high level. This satisfied most employees that the company was interested in their concerns and had evaluated the situation.

cash compensation that is typical for the role.

When looking at market data, carefully read and consider the job description that accompanies the data. Job titles will not be enough to ensure an accurate comparison to the position in the market survey. You need to be sure that the position in the survey accurately reflects the essential functions and the experience of the team member in your organization.

It is important to understand that the average for a position typically reflects employees who have been performing that job for four to six years. Therefore, it is common to bring in an entry-level employee at the 25th percentile of the survey. If you review market data and find that your employees are in the very high range of the survey, you should expect excellent performance or require them to learn new skills that will enhance the position and the impact they have within your organization. If you are in a business that is highly differentiated by talent, you will be most successful by paying at the top of a range of the market to ensure you are securing and retaining the best talent available for a particular position.

Obtain market data from an industry association where possible. This data tends to be affordable and contains positions that are aligned with the positions you have in your organization. You may be presented with requests to participate in salary surveys from various umbrella organizations or associations throughout the year. Participation takes time, but the final survey is generally available to you at a significant discount. The survey will be applicable for three or more years, and can be an invaluable tool in determining fair pay for your team. There are websites devoted to reporting salary information. One caution worth mentioning: the majority of this data is self-reported by employees and may be inflated for certain positions.

Employees don't understand the value of their total compensation package

The component that is often missing from total compensation programs is communication. Employees tend to look at their take home pay and think of that as their compensation. Often they forget their gross rate, and the amount of the pay that is being allocated for taxes and optional benefits. Employees need to consider their gross pay, as well as the statutory contributions being made on their behalf. Then add the cost of all the benefit programs provided by the organization, and you will find a total compensation number is generally 30 – 45% higher than base pay.

 Consider creating a document for your employees that will visually communicate the total package you are providing in exchange for their hard work and dedication to the business. The overview can be a simple one-page statement of the total compensation package. There are many samples found on the Internet, and many payroll companies offer basic statements as part of the service for processing payroll. Check with your insurance broker as well. Many benefit consultants will complete the statement as part of the communication of your annual program.

Action Items for compensation and benefits in your organization:

1. Understand the requirements of the Fair Labor Standards Act and insure compliance

2. Conduct annual performance evaluations and have meaningful conversations with team members

3. Evaluate resources for market comparison of employee pay

4. Provide total compensation statements to all employees

Chapter Seven

Process and Technology

Human resources have seen similar advances in the use of technology as the rest of the business world. At the same time, we find a large group of HR people stuck in the past and prefer to put their hands on paper and feel that employees can't be trusted with data entry.

Process issues that business owners identify are generally rooted in the length of time it takes to complete a task. Technology should be embraced in the human resources function and allow computers to handle the vast majority of the administration. Technology in HR should be an expected solution to process enhancement, as it will reduce costs and free up time to focus on the organizations strategic needs. While there will be a capital investment, keep in mind that technology doesn't get sick, and your data capture will be a higher quality than having entry-level employees input the information by hand.

In most organizations, technology should be used for payroll, employee files, benefit administration, and performance management. There are systems that enhance the automation of applicant tracking and attendance in smaller organizations as well. Incorporating technology may run the spectrum from using Excel spreadsheets to robust human resources information systems. The ability to maintain programs and data "in the cloud" make the implementation of human resource software as simple as turning on a switch.

Utilizing technology in the human resources function can reduce the need for human resources administrative staff, as well as allow the HR team to focus on higher-level strategic activities. Embracing technology in HR function shifts the employee population from relying on HR meeting their every need to a model that requires utilization of self-service technology. Self-service systems allow the employee to update demographic information, enroll in benefit programs, request time off etc. at a time that is most convenient to them. Ask your team to review the processes that require manual processing of data and determine if there is available technology for more efficient processing. Expect your HR function to use technology to improve processes whenever possible.

Compliance issues relating to technology

The world of technology compliance is evolving in all aspects of business. As technology impacts human resources, critical compliance issues surround the ownership and privacy of data.

- Internet access – Employees are regularly given access to the Internet. The company should monitor this access and have a written policy that covers sharing of data and downloading programs onto company systems.

- Viewing employee communication – recent policy requires that employees must be notified if their email and Internet use will be tracked and/or viewed by the company. Include this policy in the employee handbook or a separate information technology policy.

- Bring Your Own Device (BYOD) – This defines the concept that employees commonly use their own devices to connect to organizational resources. The complexity of this has arisen as a hot topic in 2014. Organizations are analyzing the cost of providing smart phones to employees with the loss of control of data security. Most major organizations are creating, defining, and implementing BYOD policies to address common issues with technology security.

- Security – Passwords protect unauthorized use of programs and data, but employees typically find the need to retain passwords cumbersome. The solution is often to have a list of passwords pinned to the cubicle wall. How should passwords be stored and shared in your organization? How will you gain access to resources if an employee terminates without providing passwords for key programs? This should be discussed and communicated to employees.

 Social media – An employer cannot restrict an employee voicing their opinion about work, said the National Labor Relations Board in 2012 when they provided guidance on employee policies on social media. At the same time there is awareness that employee conversations have never been so accessible to the entire world. All organizations should be familiar with this recommendation and adopt a similar policy.

Aligning your human resources operation with a skilled technology administrator is an important connection to have available. Many smaller organizations utilize their payroll vendor as the primary go-to resource for HR technology. Where you have a dedicated technology team for your operation, it is essential that they work closely with HR. There are compliance issues in the various areas of the employment relationship that may not seem to overlap the IT team, but are critical to incorporate in policies. At the same time, there are areas of technology that HR professionals assume are secure for data storage that may not meet required standards.

Finding HR technology solutions that make sense for my business

Implementing technology within the HR function does not have to be costly. Many of the vendors that you utilize today have solutions incorporated in their human resources products. Have meetings with the salesperson from the vendor to ensure you are embracing all that is available within their product. Where there is an additional cost, it is generally offset by the efficiencies of quicker and more accurate processing.

A little bit of training can help your administrative team create spreadsheets that can manage HR activities. Spreadsheets are often used for activities such as tracking time off and performance review dates. There are very cost effective programs available that will track FMLA, complete  OSHA forms, calculate hours worked and more. Systems can be reviewed with confidence by utilizing the Society for Human Resource Management bookstore for available options. There are many other resources available on the Internet at a price point that is affordable for even the smallest of businesses.

Eliminating Data Entry for new employees

Applicant tracking systems allow demographic information to be entered by a candidate. At the time a candidate is selected, HR indicates they are now an employee and adds the relevant information such as job title, salary and hire date to the record. All information is populated in the payroll system immediately. The system will then send the new hire all necessary paperwork necessary for their first day. Using the same technology, the new hire can complete necessary I-9, tax, and banking forms to be automatically populated in your systems.

HR will have to develop processes for employees that may not be comfortable with technology. In organizations with less sophisticated workforces it is helpful to provide a kiosk or computer in the HR office a team member can utilize. HR can be available to oversee the process and answer any questions that arise.

You need HR professionals

Employees are still human beings who require personal interaction on a regular basis. Managers will have performance issues they want to discuss. The government will continue to send countless inquiries for information, and someone with access to confidential data will need to answer the requests. Most importantly, you want to ensure that your most important resource –

your employees – are strategically aligned with your business goals and plans for the future.

An HR business partner is a term used to define the HR resource for an organization that is focused on supporting the business unit and aligning the people resources with the strategy. Your HRBP is the team member who is focused on the intersection of your business and your people. They are a partner to the management

> **It can be so easy...**
>
> An equipment organization has 65 employees. The HR manager came up through the ranks and was self-taught in the HR function. The organization was embarking on a long-term succession plan and expected HR to assist in the implementation. She said she would never have enough time with all her current duties.
>
> Upon review by the executive team, it was found that she was spending considerable time on manual activities. Ownership insisted these activities stop. They had been paying for self-service and reporting modules through payroll but she didn't trust the computer. She did not use the reporting capabilities to streamline the HR function.
>
> Through a combination of technology and an alignment of the proper function of HR, they were able to move from two full time HR team members, to one part-time HR resource. The strategy that ensured success was to move employees to self-service technology, utilize reports that were available and have the HR resource focus on strategic goals.
>
> The savings in HR salary is being used for training and coaching of team members to ensure a succession plan to sustain the business into the future.

team, a sounding board for employees and responsible

103

for the HR lifecycle from candidate selection to final separation.

The primary responsibility of the HRBP is to ensure that your people are functioning in a way that ensures successful completion of your business strategy. Technology will free up the time that allows them to put the emphasis on your business, productivity, and profitability.

Getting HR to buy into technology

Yes, HR administrators still handle a great deal of paperwork and reporting, but this is not what you should be paying them for. The role of HR should be to ensure your dollars are being spent as you intended. One example of this is to verify insurance invoices against current enrollees in the health plan. As a rule of thumb, even with the proper utilization of technology, the administrative function of the HR position will still account for 30 percent to 50 percent of an HR employee's time. Technology will allow you to move that number from the 50 to 30 percent of their time and free up 20 percent of their day for more meaningful work.

Do not accept the answer from the complacent HR administrator that they prefer to do the processing by hand. Change may not be easy for some, but without change we do not have improvements. Your HR resource may wonder what their job will be without the administrative component. You should be clear about future expectations and the desire to add value to HR beyond an administrative role. Invite your HR employee to participate in training and lead new initiatives. If moving into a more strategically focused role is not their goal, consider if you have the right talent leading your HR initiative.

Action Items for technology in your organization:

1. Review all manual processing of information and add technology where appropriate

2. Analyze technology available from current vendors – or their competitors

3. Update all policies to include Internet, Email, Social Media and BYOD

4. Consider providing a computer in HR for employee use

Chapter Eight

Outsourcing

Outsourcing is the relationship that is established by two businesses. The vendor has deep expertise and systems in a particular area that brings economies of scale to other businesses. Outsourcing typically utilizes skilled employees that understand the process and are able to deliver best-in-class service to their clients. Offshoring is the term we use when services are provided by non-US based employees. Outsourcing can involve offshoring a process, but generally we find that outsourcing for small employers is typically handled by a US based workforce.

When you consider outsourcing, don't look at it as an all-or-nothing proposition. Outsourcing all or part of the human resources function is an excellent solution for some organizations. There are many options when outsourcing, and embracing outsourcing does not mean you have to abandon the strategic component of the HR function. You are most likely outsourcing portions of the HR puzzle today as a common business practice.

When thinking about the functions of your HR team, most organizations outsource portions of the human resources administration. It is a regular practice to outsource the management of the retirement plan and payroll processing since related issues of compliance or implementation can be very cumbersome for an organization to handle internally. If you have an accounting function that claims it is easier or less expensive to process payroll internally, start a conversation and deep analysis on the topic. Recruiting is often outsourced for all the reasons we discussed in chapter five. Benefit administration has a number of steps that might be offered by your benefit broker at no additional cost. Consider asking your vendors to provide a menu of the services they can provide, and determine if you are best served with outsourcing an element of human resources administration.

Outsourcing does not let you off the hook

Understand that outsourcing does not mean that you toss your personnel issues to another entity and walk away. The best outsourcing providers will require time from your internal team. They will expect an internal conduit between the day-to-day employee activities and the agency you have selected. An outsourcing relationship is not a minimal expense, and as such is another vendor to be managed.

Your internal liaison with the outsourcing firm will need to be available to respond to questions and take time to discuss new initiatives presented by the service provider. Employees are still going to expect an internal resource especially when they don't like the answers they get from the outsourcing company. There will be internal issues that arise and a member of your organization is going to need to convey those to the outsourced vendor. There should be meetings no less than monthly between your organization and the vendor to provide feedback and suggestions for future operations. The outsourcing vendor should provide detailed notes on employee trends and how you can be an employer of choice in the future. A formal agreement will exist on rights, responsibilities, and deliverables. It will be up to your internal team to ensure these are being met and the relationship is adding the value you expected.

Outsourcing comes in various sizes and shapes to fit your business

There are a number of ways to outsource the HR function. You may choose to outsource the full function, or parts of the administration activities. Whatever solution fits best with your organizational needs, you will

want to ensure the decision is aligned with your overall strategy and goals.

There are many types of businesses that handle outsourced human resources services. To ensure common understanding, we will provide an explanation of the various types of relationships your organization might have with a vendor.

Professional Employer Organization (PEO) - The PEO will become the legal employer of your team. Employees will be paid under the federal employer identification number of the PEO and will be considered an employee of the PEO for official purposes. All tax filing, payroll obligations, unemployment etc. are the responsibility of the PEO. The PEO will handle the workers compensation insurance and be responsible for all claims payment and evaluation of injury. The employees will receive all HR services and benefits from the PEO, including paychecks, new hire orientation, benefit administration etc. This can provide a stronger benefit package to employees than you might be able to offer as an independent employer.

However, your organization will still have liability under the relationship referred to as co-employment. This means that although the employee technically works for the PEO, you have day-to-day interaction with the employees and must ensure that all employment laws are complied with. We generally see this impacting the areas of workplace harassment, pay practices, and performance management. While you and your team will still make the basic employment decision, the PEO will be able to dictate process and procedures that they find necessary to protect their employee population.

Administrative Services Only (ASO) - The relationship is similar a PEO, but does not have the co-employment component. An outside organization agrees to handle all of the administration involved with employee interactions with your organization. Employees are still paid under your corporate identity and you are responsible for all taxes and benefits. The ASO may or may not offer benefit packages depending on their structure and your requirements. Many ASO organizations are willing to administer the programs you have in place today. Typically these organizations are not involved at a strategic level and conduct the majority of interaction with your team via phone and email. The advantage is that you retain all control of HR decision-making and make the ultimate plan for the benefit programs offered and how they will be communicated within the organization.

Human Resource Practices– Consulting groups will take on the HR function in its entirety, but leave the legal obligations of your employees with your organization. This relationship provides a personal relationship created between the consultant and the organization, much like you might have with your own HR employee. The goal is to create an HR function that will look and feel like an internal department to the employees. The consulting firm will generally assign an HR administrator to the account as the primary contact. Your HR professional will typically be at your work location a few days each week, but available to all employees by phone and email during all regular business hours.

When outsourcing to a consulting firm, it is possible to arrange for both administrative and strategic support. A consulting firm should be able to assign various levels of HR professionals to your group and provide a blended monthly rate for ongoing support. This is an ideal solution as you can retain an HR administrator with two to five years of experience to work with employees on a daily basis, while engaging a strategic HR Director to work with your management team three to four hours per month or quarter as needed. With the availability of technology and the move to virtual work teams, this solution is becoming extremely popular.

The consulting firm offers the confidence that your organization will have an HR professional with access to administrative support as well as high-level HR professionals should a serious situation arise. The robust availability of talent provides your organization the right solution at the right time for a single monthly fee. This is a strong advantage to the organization that might not require a full time HR resource, or only hire a single mid-level HR professional.

Independent Consultants – Sole proprietors are plentiful in the market and seek the opportunity to support small organizations. Independent consultants are usually professionals who have left the workforce for other opportunities such as childcare, teaching or retirement. The independent contractor will be similar to the part time employee we discussed in chapter three, but they will be responsible for their own taxes, benefits and the like. The independent contractor arrangement can be thought of as a hybrid between the part-time employee and HR consulting firm. With this arrangement you will have added flexibility and a lower cost than utilizing a large consulting firm. However, you will loose the confidence of having a back up or an immediate replacement should your consultant be on vacation or close the HR consulting practice.

Vendors you work with today have outsourcing alternatives

Payroll and benefit vendors typically offer a number of services that will outsource pieces of the human resources equation. They might be in place to take administrative functions off or your team, or support an internal human resources administrator with higher-level expertise. Legal firms as well as the Society for Human Resource Management have established call services that are very helpful on a low cost, unlimited basis.

In fact, you may find that you are entitled to these services under your current agreements. Check the contract to determine what might have been agreed to during the initial sales process. Services can be quickly forgotten about as your team tries to implement the core components of the system. The sales presentation may have occurred before a decision making group and the team utilizing the system on a day-to-day basis is not aware of the increased functionality. Your team should be evaluating current vendors against the market on a regular basis to ensure they are offering the support that is standard in the market.

There are typically services available from current vendors at a minimal cost increase. This fee may be quickly offset by the timesaving for your HR team, and may provide an area of expertise that is not available to you internally. A common service offered by payroll companies is their ability to offer virtual, electronic employee files and automatically transfer data to government entities for compliance reporting. These are two areas that will save endless hours for your HR team. Having access to virtual employee files will allow managers to access information quickly without asking HR for the data.

Enlist your benefit broker to support the influx of new enrollees to a benefit plan during open enrollment. The benefit broker generates an increased commission for each new person added to the plan. They have a financial stake in making the plan easy to understand and getting people enrolled. Their annual offering may also include management of your COBRA administration and creation of the annual total compensation statements we discussed in chapter five. The benefit broker is often willing to provide these products when asked for the additional support from their clients.

Your HR team member when outsourcing

Of the vendors we have outlined that replace various parts of the HR function, rarely do they eliminate the need for an HR resource in the organization. There is always a need for employee interaction, decision making at the executive level, and management of the vendor. In considering who will be responsible, we go back to the critical questions of time, expertise, and trust. The person responsible for vendor management must have access to all HR information of all employees including ownership and must have the time and resources to manage the outside vendor.

There will have to be a member of the organization that listens to issues, makes decisions and signs documents. In many cases, an internal HR administrator will still need to complete credit verifications, mortgage applications, and other forms that require full access to employee data, including addresses and payroll information. There is always the possibility of government inquiry around compliance, and the government will expect to speak with a representative of your organization.

The individual responsible for HR must be able to hold the vendor to the deliverables that are best practice for the service being provided. For example, your payroll vendor must have all paychecks delivered the day before payday and direct deposit funds in employee accounts at midnight the day of payroll. There should be an understanding that agreements for service will be evaluated annually, if not more often. During this evaluation, consider the successes and misses over the past contract period, review of the available competition, technology enhancements and ongoing need of your organization. The recommended relationship between the vendor and your team should sit with an executive that is skilled at vendor management and understands the significance employees' play within your organization.

HR is always available with outsourcing

With full outsourcing of the HR function, management does not have to be concerned if an employee or independent contractor is on vacation, quits, or is not performing to expectations. In establishing a long-term relationship with an external organization, you will create a personal relationship with an account professional who understands the needs and culture of your business. At the same time, your HR representative will have a team supporting them to address needs at various levels that tend to arise

> **Long term partnerships...**
>
> A family business has 55 employees. Their workforce is relatively stable and committed to the organization. For many years, the accounting function handled HR administration. As the third generation took on leadership roles, they required analytical financial information and desired a strategic focus on HR. However, they did not want the complexity or expense a full time HR resource would require.
>
> After considering many options, they secured the services of a small HR consulting firm for a one-year period. The firm was able to handle payroll and all HR service through a professional that was on site two afternoons a week. Employees had access to her during all business hours via phone and email.
>
> The relationship continued for nine years. The leader of the consulting group has helped with organizational design issues, their trainer conducted various programs, and they produced compensation statements. During lean years of 2009 and 2010, the consulting firm was able to reduce their fee by utilizing administrative personnel to meet their economic concerns.
>
> They continue to work together to meet the goals of the organization and ensure HR remains a critical function.

unexpectedly. If there is a change in personnel at the outsourcing agency, you will have an immediate resource that has been trained in similar policies and procedures of the firm.

Outsourcing does not have to be permanent

Your outsourcing needs will not remain stagnant. As the number of employees and sales volumes change, your HR needs will as well. There may be times when outsourcing all or part of the HR function is the perfect solution, and times when you need the function internally managed for greater control. If you plan for quick growth that you anticipate will level off in the future, align yourself with a partner that can take on the HR function for six to twelve months while you ramp up, and then bring HR in house. This is especially effective for start up organizations that do not have expertise in HR, and need to keep their focus on the business at this stage of the organizational life cycle.

Outsourcing portions of HR administration is very advantageous in the areas of retirement plan management and payroll. There will be different needs as the organization changes, but that can be evaluated. The vendor you select today may not be the best fit in two years, and making a change is not as cumbersome as some executives think. While change is never easy, managing the process is possible and valuable when a new resource is identified.

Selecting an outsourcing partner

It is common for business owners to feel overwhelmed and begin the vendor search with national providers. However, small businesses can become a small fish in a large pond and find their needs are not served in the way you might hope. Look for local businesses that are aligned with your strategy and will see your organization as a valuable client. You must check references and ensure quality, but generally a smaller organization will create the familial relationship many small business owners strive for.

As a business executive, you will be aligned with a number of trusted advisors that can make recommendations to outsourced options. It is common for your payroll service, benefit broker, accountant, and attorney to be aware of various resources that provide HR services and would be appropriate for your organization. Your trusted advisors might even offer programs that you weren't aware of, or they didn't know that you were interested in. These advisors should have partners in all areas of HR administration they can recommend for you to consider.

Start with a few sales meetings to learn the services that are available. This will help you refine your requirements and consider offerings you may not have been aware of. Create a formal request for proposal that will ensure the vendors are giving you solutions that can be compared on an even playing field. Don't be tempted by the lowest offer, and if you like what a higher priced organization had to offer call and determine if you are getting additional value that will transfer to other parts of the business in a positive way. There is generally room to negotiate, so lay the options out to your first choice and see if they are willing to move their fee to be more competitive if necessary.

The contract

It is essential that you have a formal agreement with the contractor spelling out how the fees will be billed and what expenses the vendor is allowed to incur on your behalf. The agreement should include the fees anticipated for communication, postage, and travel expense. It is common for an outsourced HR function to provide food for events and then bill the company on a monthly basis. The authorization for these expenses should be very clear. The contractor should be required to maintain injury and professional liability insurance at agreed upon amounts. Many national providers may not be flexible in their agreement, but you should know what is and is not included. Smaller vendors will typically adapt portions of their standard agreement to your needs.

It is common for you to sign a power of attorney for consultants. This will provide the authority to submit government documents on your behalf, sign agreements for company events, generate purchase orders, and other actions as a representative of the company. The authority given should be clearly spelled out in the agreement. For example, you may have a consultant represent you at an unemployment hearing, but they need the authority to do so.

A strong outsourcing agreement is critical to ensure the outsourcing agency or consultant will stand behind the advice given that is so prevalent in the HR function. Ask for assurances of how administrative issues will be dealt with. Mistakes will happen in payroll and benefit administration, and it should be clearly determined at the start of the relationship how these issues will be resolved between the two organizations. If there are fees or penalties incurred, which organization will bear the cost of correcting the error?

The agreement is generally complex and financial in nature, so we often see outsourcing aligned with the CFO. It's critical to understand your organization's outsourcing goals in selecting the right person to manage the relationship. Consider the same pros and cons we discussed in chapter three relating to the reporting structure of human resources.

Moving to outsourcing to save money

Overall cost savings should not be the primary

consideration when evaluating movement to an outsourced provider. In two decades of evaluation, we typically find less than a 15 percent variation in the cost of an in-house versus outsourcing HR solutions. Extreme cost savings will generally come with a move to automation and call center type operations. Many small business owners find this to be at odds with their culture, and will move toward a solution that is more personal in nature. This will require a cost similar to the internal solution, but provide the opportunity to align your HR offering with experts in technology and best practices.

Ultimately you must consider the internal cost of HR including all benefits and taxes of your team member against the external cost being proposed. Consider the additional space required for the HR team, office supplies, training requirements, travel to events etc. in addition to the salary and benefits.

Do not minimize the risk your organization takes on if HR activities are not managed properly. If you consider the total cost of having high-level HR, administration, recruiting, training and development, and a compensation expert all on your team, then there is certainly a cost savings. The ability for a small organization to have multiple levels of HR professionals available, and the confidence that there will always be skilled back up is a very attractive advantage to outsourcing.

Consider growth when evaluating the fees from the outsourced provider. If you add ten employees this year, does the fee increase? Is the outsourcing fee based on the salary of your employees? Do you plan to fill key management positions in the next year? If these answers are yes, understand that every time you increase salaries your fees to the PEO will increase. The fee structure must be negotiated in outsourcing agreements or the arrangement can become expensive very quickly.

Telling employees there is now a third party involved

If the ultimate decision is to outsource all or part of the HR function, your first conversation should be with the current member of your team handling human resources activities. In the best scenario, this person will have been involved in the evaluating potential outsource providers. They will understand the need to utilize an outside vendor and be able to "sell" it internally to the team.

Focus on the fact that you need your HR resource to be a business partner first. The expectation is that the HR outsourced vendor will add value to the organization and be able to save resources by understanding unemployment, workers compensation, recruiting, file management etc. HR in the future should be focused on working with managers to turn around employees with performance issues, or terminate employees when that is the appropriate decision. Be emphatic that these actions are going to be the focus of HR going forward, which is why the decision was made to outsource administration.

When introducing the new vendor, be sure to explain how they will interact with your organization and whom the employee should see internally if there is an issue. Provide an internal resource if there is a matter so confidential they are not comfortable dealing with an outside vendor. Explain that the team approach the vendor can offer will answer questions and address issues quickly and efficiently, and other resources that might be available such as 24/7 Internet access to data. Your employees will be less concerned with the outsourcing relationship once they are comfortable their needs will be met.

OUTSOURCING

Action Items for outsourcing HR in your organization:

1. Evaluate current vendors and ensure you are utilizing all services included in your agreement

2. Determine which HR activities, if any, should be outsourced

3. Discuss the idea of full outsourcing with your leadership team

4. Conduct two or three meetings with PEO's or ASO's to understand HR offerings and determine if they are appropriate for your operation

Chapter Nine

Pulling it all together

How you will embrace human resources in your organization can be a daunting and tedious task. We start with the issues that are of highest concern to the business owner, and provide tips and trick to address the issues. The goal of this book is to help small and middle market business owners understand solutions that are available to embrace various aspects of human resources functionality.

HR should be an asset to your management team, not a headache keeping you up at night. Bringing the appropriate level of human resources support into your organization and addressing common topics head on is an essential part of leadership. There are no right or wrong answers to your questions of how HR will fit into your organization.

Challenge your executives to think about the strategic plan, and how people play into achieving those goals. Review the budget and determine how much of your top line revenue or bottom line expense is impacted by the administration and quality of the employees on your team. There are likely line items that can be reduced with the focus of a dedicated HR resource. A common example would be reducing or eliminating the use of outside recruiters and make this the responsibility of your HR administrator. You might achieve this through the addition of an HR professional, or additional training for your current resource. With the savings of recruiting alone you may pay for your HR function the first year.

While it is always tempting to look at expense reduction, also consider the opportunity cost overlooked with accountants, engineers and plant managers spending time on HR functions. Are you loosing top talent to the competition because you don't have a benefit package that has been evaluated against the market, or the candidates are not being courted in a way that establishes your business as an employer of choice? Executives are taxed and under pressure to meet goals. Handling HR may be one distraction too many and is keeping critical business goals from being addressed.

There are some organizations where the HR team functions as the rule enforcers and are not aligned with the business strategy. There is a perception that HR leaders keep managers from running the day-to-day operation with rules and a focus on employees that defies logic. This is unacceptable. HR is not a part of your team for the purpose of creating and enforcing rules. Finding the right HR solution is complex, but not impossible.

There must be a culture fit between HR and the rest of the organization, and a place for risk/reward conversations to take place. We have evaluated a number of solutions both internally and externally to support your organization in this goal.

You should expect that HR is aligned with your mission, understands the strategic goals, and works to enact initiatives that will drive these forward. HR must be flexible and adaptable, and not locked into the current system and processes that they are unable to move as the organization uncovers new opportunities or threats. As such, we expect HR to use rules as a guideline for decision-making, not a codebook from which deviation is impossible. Businesses must be nimble and ready to move as the market or other forces require attention. Your HR function should be no different.

Conduct an HR assessment to ensure the team member responsible for compliance of human resources activities is meeting expectations. Ideally, hire a skilled HR professional or employment attorney to conduct the audit. The fees paid should be offset by the knowledge gained and the protection against government action. A good HR assessment will provide training and best practices for your HR team. If an outside resource is not possible, conduct a self-audit to evaluate the current state of HR and find resources to answer questions or verify issues that are uncovered.

Every business relies on people to get their product to the customer. Whether it is through sales, research and development, production, or shipping, your people are what set you apart. The additional time spent with the HR function will be productive time focused on driving your business forward. What is the cost to the organization of buying capital equipment only to find that the local talent pool does not have the skills to utilize the functionality of the equipment you are so excited about? Your HR professional should be part of the conversation to build awareness early on in the decision making process.

Evaluate the culture of your business and bring in a person or organization that will support that growth and maintain the culture you want. Your HR resource needs to be available when the unexpected occurs, and that should be a consideration in your final evaluation of next steps in the human resources puzzle.

The five issues that rise to the top of the survey will not go away for the small business owner. Issues will occur, but alignment with the right resources will provide comfort that they can be handled quickly and professionally – allowing you to get back to the business of running your business.

PULLING IT ALL TOGETHER

About the Author

Lori Kleiman is a human resources speaker, author, and consultant with more than 25 years of experience advising companies on HR issues. Her background as human resources professional and consultant gives her unique insight on how executives and business owners can address common HR topics to meet business goals.

Lori's business career started as the HR Manager and ended as the VP of Operations for a family owned business. K&S PhotoGraphics. K&S employed 250 employees in five states with sales in excess of thirteen million dollars.

A frequent speaker on a wide range of HR topics, Lori's programs are designed to provide critical HR updates and best practices to small businesses. She also runs mastermind groups for HR managers and consultants to stay connected with and add value to the HR profession.

Sharing her love of HR with adult learners, Lori Kleiman is an adjunct faculty member at Oakton Community College, Illinois Institute of Technology, and DePaul University.

Previously, Lori founded HRpartners; a boutique HR consulting firm that was acquired by Arthur J. Gallagher & Co. in 2007. Lori continued with Gallagher through the summer of 2013 to lead the firm's HR consulting practice before branching out again as an independent consultant, author, and speaker.

Lori has a master's degree in human resources, is

certified as Senior Professional in Human Resources (SPHR) by the HR Certification Institute and is a member of the National Speakers Association.

She lives in Glenview Illinois with her husband Andy, and has three grown children.

Learn more about Lori at www.hrtopics.com.

Also by the author:

Written to both CEO's and HR Leaders encouraging conversation around goals and bringing meaningful human resources into every organization

Companion workbook and webinar schedule providing tips and tricks of implementing the suggestions in the text.

BOTH TITLES AVAILABLE AT:

WWW.HRTOPICS.COM

HR YOU CAN USE!

Made in the USA
San Bernardino, CA
19 November 2014